Cultural & Social History

THE JOURNAL OF THE SOCIAL HISTORY SOCIETY

Volume 6, Issue 4

Special Issue
Partition of India: The Human Dimension

Cultural and Social History

Recent epistemological challenges have shaken the core assumptions of many historians. 'Culture' is now seen as a product of social practice, and therefore at the heart of society itself. *Cultural and Social History*, the official peer-reviewed journal of the Social History Society (SHS), aims to address disciplinary shifts between social and cultural historians. The journal emphasizes the ways the 'social' and 'culture' are inextricable and enable a deeper understanding of each other.

Cultural and Social History: The Journal of the Social History Society (ISSN 1478-0038 print; ISSN 1478-0046 online) is published four times per year by Berg Publishers, 1st Floor, Angel Court, 81 St Clements Street, Oxford, OX4 1AW UK. Four parts form a volume.

2009 Subscription rates
Print
Institutional (1 year): £173/US$338; (2 year) £277/$541
Single issues: £30/US$60

Online only
Institutional (1 year): £147/$287; (2 year): £236/$459
Free online subscription for institutional print subscribers.
Full colour images are available online.
Access your electronic subscription through www.ingenta.com

2009 Membership rates
Membership of the Social History Society is open to all interested individuals, not just professional scholars and students. To download the membership form go to www.socialhistory.org.uk

Individual: £40, Postgraduate: £15, Partner: £18
Members of the Social History Society receive the journal as part of their membership fee.
See http://www.socialhistory.org.uk or http://www.bergpublishers.com/JournalsHomepage/CulturalandSocialHistory/JournalMenu/CulturalSocialHistorySubscriptions/tabid/3511/Default.aspx

Orders and payment
Turpin Distribution handle the distribution of this journal. Institutional orders accompanied with payment (cheques made payable to Turpin Distribution) should be sent directly to Turpin Distribution, Stratton Business Park, Pegasus Drive, Biggleswade, Bedfordshire, SG18 8TQ, UK.
Tel: +44 (0)1767 604951. Fax: +44 (0)1767 601640. E-mail: custserv@turpin-distribution.com

Enquiries
Julia Hall, Managing Editor
email: jhall@bergpublishers.com
Production: Ian Critchley
email: icritchley@bergpublishers.com
Advertising and subscriptions: Corina Kapinos
email: ckapinos@bergpublishers.com

Articles appearing in this journal are abstracted and indexed in America: History and Life; the British Humanities Index; Historical Abstracts; International Bibliography of Book Reviews; International Bibliography of Periodical Literature; PAIS International; Linguistics and Language Behavior Abstracts; Scopus; Social Services Abstracts; and Sociological Abstracts

Berg Publishers is a member of CrossRef.

Submissions
Submissions should be sent in electronic format (either Word or Rich Text Format) to culturalsocialhistory@bergpublishers.com

Reprints
Copies of individual articles may be obtained from the publishers at the appropriate fees. Write to: Berg Publishers, 1st Floor, Angel Court, 81 St Clements Street, Oxford OX4 1AW, UK

Typeset by Avocet Typesetting, Chilton, Aylesbury, Bucks
Printed in the UK

The Social History Society

Objectives

The society was founded in 1976 to encourage the study of the history of society and cultures by teaching, research, publication and other appropriate means. Since then it has organized a conference annually and acted to represent the interests of social and cultural history and of social and cultural historians both within higher education and in the wider community. The society is based in the UK but is concerned with social history internationally and in all its broadest forms. It welcomes not only contributions and members from overseas, but also historians and interested individuals from both inside and outside the formal academic community. It actively seeks to maintain links with other historical societies and bodies, nationally and internationally.

Cultural & Social History

THE JOURNAL OF THE
SOCIAL HISTORY SOCIETY

Volume 6, Issue 4

CONTENTS

AUTHORS' BIOGRAPHIES

Paul Ashmore is a PhD student in the Department of History, University of Sheffield. He is currently completing a thesis entitled 'Placing Ideas and Ideas of Place: Visions of Empire Self-Sufficiency, c.1912–1930'. More broadly, he is interested in the interplay of ideas, practices and place.

Virginia Berridge is Director of the Centre for History in Public Health at the London School of Hygiene and Tropical Medicine. Her most recent book is *Marketing Health: Smoking and the Discourse of Public Health in Britain, 1945–2000* (Oxford, 2007).

Alexander Cowan is Reader in History at Northumbria University. He has written widely on early modern Venetian social history and is the author of *Marriage, Manners and Mobility in Early Modern Venice* (2007).

Sean P. Holmes is based at Brunel University, West London. His research focuses on the politics of cultural production and, more particularly, trade unionism in the American entertainment industry.

Ananya Jahanara Kabir is Senior Lecturer at the School of English, University of Leeds, and the author of *Territory of Desire: Representing the Valley of Kashmir* (Minneapolis, MN, and New Delhi, 2009). She is currently working on a monograph entitled *Beyond the Nation: Partition Effects and Modern South Asia*.

Ravinder Kaur is Associate Professor at the University of Copenhagen, Denmark. She is the author of *Since 1947: Partition Narratives among Punjabi Migrants of Delhi* (Delhi, 2007) and editor of *Religion, Violence and Political Mobilisation in South Asia* (London and Delhi, 2005)

Stuart Mitchell has been involved with the Open University for the past fifteen years - as academic consultant, lecturer and tutor. His first book, *The Brief and Turbulent Life of Modernising Conservatism*, was published in 2006.

Clare Rose is the 2009 Women's Library Douie Research Fellow, London Metropolitan University, with a project on 'The Politics of Appearance: Feminist Self-presentation in the 1970s'. The monograph *Making, Selling and Wearing Boys' Clothes in Late-Victorian England*, based on her PhD, will be published by Ashgate in late 2009.

Judith Rowbotham is a reader, specializing in historical legal and criminal justice studies, at Nottingham Trent University, and a co-founder and Director of the SOLON consortium. Her interests include the popular presentation of the law in the nineteenth and twentieth centuries, via newsprint and other printed sources.

Willemijn Ruberg is a lecturer in cultural history at the Department of History, Utrecht University. She has published on the history of autobiographical writing and correspondence, as well as mourning dress and emotions in the eighteenth and nineteenth centuries. Currently she is working on an edited collection entitled *Sexed Sentiments: Interdisciplinary Perspectives on Gender and Emotion* (Amsterdam, forthcoming).

Vanita Sharma has taught history at Oxford University, the School of Oriental and African Studies (SOAS) and the Lahore University of Management Sciences (LUMS). Her doctoral research examined the creation of collective memory about the 1947 Partition of British India and founding of Pakistan. She has supported a number of peace initiatives between India and Pakistan, written articles for Indian and Pakistani national newspapers and in 2005 held a WISCOMP Scholar of Peace Fellowship.

Adrian Shubert has published widely on the social and cultural history of modern Spain and was awarded the Order of Civil Merit by King Juan Carlos. He is Professor of History and Associate Vice-President International at York University, Toronto, Canada.

Lata Singh is currently Fellow, Indian Institute of Advanced Study, Shimla, and Associate Professor, Department of History, Maitreyi College, Delhi University. She has been a British Academy visiting fellow, an affiliated fellow to Nehru Memorial Museum and Library, New Delhi, and a research awardee of the University Grant Commission. Her broad area of research is gender, modern and contemporary history and theatre. Her book *Play-House of Power: Theatre in Colonial India* (Oxford and New Delhi) is forthcoming in 2009. She was guest editor of the *Indian Historical Review* (the biannual journal of the Indian Council of Historical Research, New Delhi) on the special theme 'Issues of Gender: Colonial and Post-colonial India', July–December 2008.

Mark B. Smith is Lecturer in Modern European History at Durham University. His published research concerns the urban housing programme in the Soviet Union, and he also works on other Stalin- and Khrushchev-era topics.

Ian Talbot was educated at Royal Holloway, University of London, from where he graduated in 1976 and obtained a PhD in 1981. He is presently Professor in History at the University of Southampton, where he is Head of Discipline and Director of the Centre for Imperial and Post-colonial Studies. He has published extensively on the Colonial Punjab, the 1947 Partition of India and the post-independence history of Pakistan. His most recent publications are *Pakistan: A Modern History* (London, 2009) and, jointly with Gurharpal Singh, *The Partition of India* (Cambridge, 2009).

Pippa Virdee is Senior Lecturer in History at De Montfort University, Leicester. She is the convener for the Punjab Research Group. She is the author of *Coming to Coventry: Stories from the South Asian Pioneers* (Coventry, 2006). She has also written several articles on the impact of Partition in the Punjab and is currently working on an edited volume with Panikos Panayi, *Refugees and the End of Empire* (Basingstoke, forthcoming).

Fiona Williamson is a lecturer in early modern history at the University of East Anglia. Her PhD thesis examines social relations in early modern England with special attention to space, agency and identity.

Anticapitalism and Culture
Radical Theory and Popular Politics

Jeremy Gilbert

'This book convincingly argues that cultural studies can only reinvigorate itself by connecting its arguments on culture to the politics of the great oppositional movement of the twenty-first century, the alter-globalisation or anti-capitalist movement. Essential reading for cultural studies thinkers and anyone interested in culture and anti-capitalism'.

Tim Jordan, Open University

What does 'anticapitalism' really mean for the politics and culture of the twenty-first century?

Anticapitalism is an idea which, despite going global, remains rooted in the local, persisting as a loose collection of grassroots movements and actions. Anticapitalism needs to develop a coherent and cohering philosophy, something which cultural theory and the intellectual legacy of the New Left can help to provide, notably through the work of key radical thinkers, such as Ernesto Laclau, Stuart Hall, Antonio Negri, Gilles Deleuze and Judith Butler.

Anticapitalism and Culture argues that there is a strong relationship between the radical tradition of cultural studies and the new political movements which try to resist corporate globalization. Indeed, the two need each other: whilst theory can shape and direct the huge diversity of anticapitalist activism, the energy and sheer political engagement of the anticapitalist movement can breathe new life into cultural studies.

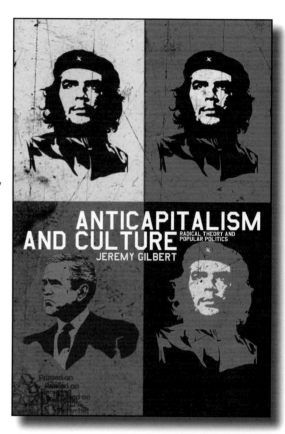

Sept 08 • 224pp
PB 978 1 84520 230 9 **£16.99 $29.95**
HB 978 1 84520 229 3 **£55.00 $109.95**

PARTITION OF INDIA: THE HUMAN DIMENSION

INTRODUCTION

Ian Talbot
University of Southampton

The British transferred power to the two dominions of India and Pakistan on 14 and 15 August 1947.[1] The demand for a separate Muslim homeland had only been raised by the Muslim League seven years earlier. It followed a two year period of Congress rule in India's provinces, which had been given full autonomy under the terms of the 1935 Government of India Act. This experience aroused exaggerated fears that Muslim culture and the community's economic interests would be endangered by a Hindu Raj when the British departed India. The creation of a Muslim homeland was, however, by no means a foregone conclusion, because the Muslim League traditionally had little influence in those areas of India which formed the heartland of a future Pakistan state. It thus needed to beat off regional rivals, such as the Punjab Unionist Party, as well as convince the British and the Congress about the credibility of its Pakistan demand.

The Second World War greatly aided the Muslim League's advance.[2] Future constitutional advance was postponed on the pretext of respecting Muslim political opinion, as the war clouds of a Japanese invasion loomed over the subcontinent. The incarceration of virtually all of the Congress leadership in the wake of the 1942 Quit India movement also created a vacuum which the Muslim League was able to fill. Most importantly, the unpopular army recruitment and agricultural policies that the Unionist government had to carry out in the key Punjab province undermined its standing with the rural population. The Punjabi cultivators had previously kept the Muslim League at arm's length. From 1944 onwards, they increasingly saw the League as a better vehicle for their interests than the discredited Unionist Party. Moreover, Jinnah's refusal at the 1945 Simla Conference to countenance any Punjabi Muslim representation on an expanded Viceroy's Executive Council outside of the Muslim League encouraged many of the Unionist Party's landed supporters to opportunistically shift their allegiance.

The Muslim League's wartime advance was accompanied by increasing tension as religion became a major focus of political identity. In the context of the Indian subcontinent, the latter process is known as communalism.[3] This was especially

Address for correspondence: Ian Talbot, History, School of Humanities, University of Southampton, Southampton, SO17 1BJ, UK. E-mail: I.A.Talbot@soton.ac.uk

Cultural and Social History, Volume 6, Issue 4, pp. 403–410 © The Social History Society 2009
DOI 10.2752/147800409X466254

marked in the Punjab, where the important Sikh minority population had no desire to be included in a future state of Pakistan. This in part resulted from the fact that the politicization of Sikh identity from the late nineteenth century onwards had been forged around selective replaying of historical community memories of Mughal and Afghan eighteenth century repression. The 1946 provincial elections made Pakistan a possibility as the Muslim League achieved a breakthrough not only in the Punjab but also in the other centres of Muslim population. Without this advance, the credibility of its separatist demands would have been shot to pieces. Despite winning an overwhelming majority of the Muslim seats, it was unable, however, to form a government in the Punjab, where an 'unholy alliance' of the Unionists, the Congress and the main Sikh Party (Akali Dal) was formed. Violence initially broke out on a large scale in August 1946 not in the Punjab but in Bengal, the other main Muslim majority province. The role of the Muslim League provincial government in directing this outbreak remains controversial, but there is no dispute that it was occasioned by Jinnah's Call for Direct Action in response to the collapse of the Cabinet Mission proposals and the British decision to form an interim All-India government without the Muslim League's inclusion. The violence in Calcutta, which resulted in around 4,000 deaths, led to a chain reaction of riots in Bengal and Bihar. The worsening situation was the backdrop to the replacement of the Viceroy, Lord Wavell, by Mountbatten. The latter was tasked by the Attlee administration with bringing down the curtain on the British Raj. By the time of Mountbatten's arrival in India on 22 March 1947, the focus of the violence had shifted from Bengal to the Punjab. The province was placed under Direct Governor's rule after widespread violence in the Rawalpindi Division had accompanied the resignation of the Unionist coalition at the beginning of the month.

Mountbatten had intended to resurrect the Cabinet Mission proposals for a federal India. British officials were unanimously pessimistic about a Pakistan state's future economic prospects. The agreement to an Indian Union contained in the Cabinet Mission proposals had been initially accepted by the Muslim League as the grouping proposals gave considerable autonomy in the Muslim majority areas. Moreover, there was the possibility of withdrawal and thus acquiring Pakistan by the backdoor after a ten year interval. The worsening communal situation and extensive soundings with Indian political figures convinced Mountbatten within a month of his arrival that partition was, however, the only way to secure a speedy and smooth transfer of power. Nevertheless, it was not easy for him to sell this policy to Nehru, who had been committed throughout his career to Indian unity. Furthermore, Nehru feared that the creation of Pakistan might hasten a more general Balkanization of the subcontinent. It was something of a tour de force on Mountbatten's part to get the Indian leaders to all agree to his 3 June Partition Plan. Not even the Muslim League leadership was particularly pleased by the outcome, as it had previously hoped that the whole of the Punjab and Bengal would be included in the new Muslim homeland. While some in the Congress ranks were glad to rid themselves of the 'Muslim problem' and indeed cynically believed that Pakistan would fail, for leaders such as Nehru and Gandhi Partition represented a blow to their long-term commitment to Indian unity.

Once the 3 June Plan was agreed, Mountbatten put in place the administrative machinery to oversee the division of the subcontinent. A Partition Council pored over the issue of the division of the assets of undivided India between the two future dominions. A Boundary Commission headed by the British lawyer Sir Cyril Radcliffe was appointed to demarcate the boundaries of the new states in the partitioned provinces of Bengal and the Punjab.[4] If these tasks were not enough, the Indian Army had to be divided and arrangements drawn up regarding the future of the 600 or so Indian Princely States following the lapse of British paramountcy. Mountbatten controversially brought forward the date for the British departure from June 1948 to August 1947. This has led some historians to 'blame' him for the severe dislocation which surrounded Partition.[5] In his defence it could be argued that the gravity of the situation indicated that any delay would have stored up greater trouble. Moreover, the Partition process was undermined by the lack of trust and animosity between the major parties. The Partition Council proceedings occurred amidst much bitterness and animosity. While deliberations in New Delhi ground on in an atmosphere of mutual recrimination, reports from the localities indicated that weapons were being stockpiled and preparations for what a later generation would term 'ethnic cleansing' were under way in the Punjab.

The fact that the boundary line in the Punjab and Bengal was not announced until two days after the British handover of power undoubtedly contributed to the general air of uncertainty and foreboding. The Boundary Commission, which was supposed to oversee a judicial award, had been thoroughly politicized in its proceedings. Representatives of the main parties made mutually incompatible claims in its public sittings. In the press, statements were issued threatening violence to defend vested community interests. The fact that 'other factors' as well as contiguous population majorities were part of the Commission's remit opened up the possibilities of counter-claims. The provincial capital of the Punjab, Lahore, was, for example, claimed by the Muslim League because it had a Muslim majority, but by the Congress and the Sikhs because of their economic contribution to its wealth and its historical associations with their rule. The Bengal Boundary Commission was less contentious, as it was clear from the outset that Calcutta would be awarded to India. Nevertheless, similar politicking accompanied its deliberations.

Officials and politicians alike were taken aback by the violence and social upheaval which accompanied Partition. Rather than ending the violence and distrust which had stalked India, it sparked off massive disturbances, especially in the Punjab region, the historic centre of recruitment for the Indian Army and an area which was awash with weapons in 1947. The number of casualties remains a matter of dispute, with figures being claimed that range from 200,000 to 2 million victims.[6] Rival community and national historical discourses attempt to displace the blame for the killings. Many of these were carried out with military precision and were not spontaneous hot-blooded assaults, although this element was also present. Large scale rape and abduction of women accompanied the killing and looting. Women were especially targeted, not only because of their vulnerability but more importantly because they were seen as upholding community 'honour'. As many as 100,000 women from all communities were abducted during the disturbances. The Indian and Pakistan states were subsequently to devote great efforts to 'recover' women. These on occasion involved a second violence as women were wrenched away from the homes and children they had given birth to on the other side of the border. Moreover, they were not always welcomed back by their families because of their 'dishonouring'.

The massacres led to an unprecedented mass migration of population in the days which followed the British departure. Within less than two months, over nine million people had migrated in the Punjab alone. Elsewhere in the subcontinent, dislocation continued, although less intensely, for months. Indeed the greatest migration in the Bengal region occurred not in 1947 but in 1950. Ultimately, Bengal was to suffer the greatest dislocation as waves of refugees flooded across its new international borders whenever there were riots in the region or elsewhere in the subcontinent. Partition was thus to result in the greatest movement of population in a twentieth century that was marked by refugee flights in the face of war, civil unrest and natural disaster.[7]

The newly independent states had to address the major problems of safely moving, feeding and housing the flood of refugees. In the Punjab region, but not in Bengal, they drew up plans for the exchange of both land and immovable property. There was also large-scale provision of refugee housing in satellite towns and refugee colonies. Grants were provided for refugees to start small businesses or to acquire educational qualifications. The state responses were accompanied by widespread corruption as refugees, officials and locals sought to acquire abandoned property and goods. Many refugees were to subsequently claim that it was their own self-reliance rather than state assistance that enabled their shattered lives to be resumed after the massive upheaval. Stereotypes of the self-reliant and entrepreneurial Punjabi fed into both the official accounts of refugee rehabilitation and the family memories which have been recently recovered from Partition survivors.

Partition scholarship was initially dominated, however, not by concerns with the social consequences of its aftermath, but by 'high politics' accounts of the constitutional negotiations between the British and the Congress and Muslim League representatives.[8] The emphasis was on why India was divided in 1947. Some of the most extreme views focused around Jinnah's role. While he was lionized in Pakistan, he was demonized in India. The rise of Hindu nationalist ideology in the past three decades has resulted in increasing criticism within India of Nehru's role in independence.[9] Critics have seen him as being too willing to accept the 'parting British gift' of Partition. Debates also swirl around the Mountbatten viceroyalty and the extent to which he was partial to Indian interests. This has been a long-standing claim in Pakistan, which has been recently revived by British and American critics of Mountbatten.[10] They have castigated his 'shameful flight' and maintained that his 'ignorance' of India and personal impulsiveness contributed to the upheavals surrounding Partition. The 'high politics' approach left little space for a consideration of the human costs of Partition, although these were reflected soon after independence in the fictional works of such 'progressive' writers as Saadat Hasan Manto, Krishan Chander and Rajinder Singh Bedi.

The term partition was rarely used in Pakistan because of its connotations of secession and its usage in Hindu nationalist thinking. Historical discourses focused instead on the themes of freedom and independence. The silences about Partition in Pakistan were assisted by the relative ease of the assimilation of Muslim refugees from East Punjab. The influential Hindu refugee community in India, on the other hand, ensured that the fact that independence came hand in hand with Partition was never totally lost sight of. Indeed the nostalgic remembrance of pre-Partition Lahore has become not only a cliché but also a symbol of the wider losses of Partition. The imbalance between Pakistani and Indian writing spreads much more widely, however, than the usage of the term partition. The needs of nation building and the impact of a succession of authoritarian governments in Pakistan have stifled both analytical and creative reflection. Official histories have been dominated by understanding the achievement of Pakistan as a result of the existence of 'two nations' in the subcontinent. Islam, these accounts insist, had given birth to a distinctive Muslim social order that was fundamentally at odds with Hindu society. The demand for a separate state as British rule drew to its close was a natural 'expression' of this reality. The other major theme of Pakistani writings revolves around the charismatic role of *Quaid-e-Azam* ('Great Leader') Mohammad Ali Jinnah. He continues to form the focus of a cottage industry of historical scholarship which crowds out other approaches to the division of the subcontinent. Significantly, the transformation in approach to Partition which has occurred within the last two decades has been dominated by scholarship focused around the Indian experience.

The emphasis has shifted from explaining Partition to examining its consequences and its aftermath for ordinary people. The feminist writers and activists Urvashi Butalia and Ritu Menon played a leading part in this concern with Partition's 'history from beneath'.[11] They opened up for the first time the silences in the historical discourse with respect to the impact of Partition on Untouchables, women and children. They also revealed the way in which women were victims of the processes of both abduction and state recovery. Indeed a gendered dimension of Partition has been central to its reshaping. Practitioners of the 'new history' of Partition have turned to first-hand testimonies to address these questions. Literature has also been used as a source to deconstruct the meanings of Partition. The role of interdisciplinary work has thus come to lie at the heart of the evolution of Partition Studies. The personal, family, community and regional ramifications of Partition are so significant that only by drawing on insights from ethnographic study, literature, history and politics can they begin to be addressed.

The 'new history' has not been without its methodological critics.[12] They have questioned the veracity of first-hand accounts, both because of faulty remembrance and the distortions arising from the impact of collective memory on personal recollections. The issue has also been raised as to whether literary accounts can be utilized as sources for subaltern experiences, given that they are elite 'literate' productions. Artistic representation, moreover, could equally impact on first-hand testimony along with community and official texts. Nevertheless, its ability to provide a nuanced understanding of the events of 1947 which transcends attempts at a historical 'blame game' or resting accounts in terms of an essentialized religious identity has led respected scholars such as Mushirul Hasan to see literature as a rich resource for understanding Partition.[13]

The new historical approach was clearly evident by the end of the 1990s. This was seen not just in academic circles, but also in the popular impact in India of Urvashi Butalia's pioneering text *The Other Side of Silence*. The public sphere now reflected much more openly on Partition in terms of plays, such as *Aur Kitne Tukde* ('How many more fragments?'), which is the focus of one of this issue's articles, public art and documentary film than had been the case previously. The earlier reticence was exemplified by Indian cinema's lack of engagement with the Partition theme. There is growing evidence that in India the increased space for the cultural representation of Partition is breaking down the previous divide between public memory of independence as 'freedom' and private and personal recollection of the 'suffering' of Partition which accompanied it.

The articles in this volume reflect the 'new history' approach to Partition. They possess its urge to put a human face on the bald statistics of abductions, deaths and property losses. The contributions not only represent the current stage of scholarship, but also seek to push out further its boundaries. The imbalance in the historiography between Pakistani and India-centred accounts noted by many scholars is redressed here through the studies of Ananya Kabir and Pippa Virdee. Besides, interdisciplinary work that is only beginning to emerge is given central attention in several articles here. Visual history and representations of human drama surfacing from the creative arts such as theatre are integrated in core ways by Lata Singh and Ananya Kabir. Both authors reach novel conclusions about concepts of memory, loss, pain and agency through the use of the rich mediums of play and art. This collection also breaks new ground by offering comparative perspectives from the wholly European experience of the Holocaust. Several studies here rework the models thrown up by Holocaust studies on the centrality of 'loss', 'remembrance' and 'repression'. If many wished to heal from the trauma of Partition, an equal number showed the zeal to forget and move on.

Lata Singh's contribution, for example, raises questions about theatre and how its representation of the Partition-related violence compares with the now well-established insights from literature. It also reveals importantly that the play *Aur Kitne Tukde* received a different reception from Punjabi than from Delhi audiences. The silences surrounding the histories of lived experience come out clearly in the ways in which the production itself impacted on some of the actors. It was only when they became involved with it that stories of the migration and upheaval were shared from within their own families.

Pippa Virdee also pushes out academic boundaries when her article deals with the neglected history of Muslim women's experiences of Partition. There are only a handful of accounts of this topic. The literature ever since the pioneering studies by Urvashi Butalia and Ritu Menon has been dominated by accounts drawn from women in the Hindu and Sikh communities. Virdee's article thus provides much original material which is drawn from refugee families in the Pakistan Punjab.

Ananya Kabir provides another highly original contribution, which again focuses on the neglected Pakistan experience of Partition. She picks up on the centrality of visual production of language scripts in what has been a highly contested process of Pakistani identity formation. Calligraphy's role in establishing a modernist identity for the nation state is considered in fresh and challenging ways.

The differentiation in refugee experiences lies at the heart of Ravinder Kaur's contribution. This is now recognized as an emerging element in Partition studies. The ability to recover the losses of forced migration is understood both in terms of the social and cultural capital of the migrants and the post-colonial state's differential treatment of refugees according to their caste and class status. The Punjab experience was not of course the only element in the refugee rehabilitation process, although both community and state stereotypes derived from this have crowded out regional differentiation which is as marked as the intra-Punjab variations referred to in the text.

Vanita Sharma's original contribution rests on her examination of how memories about Partition have been transmitted across generations. Like much of the 'new history' of Partition, the article focuses on a reflective use of oral history sources. This provides a nuanced reading of individual and collective experiences. The important point of silences, first raised by Urvashi Butalia, is addressed. In some families, Sharma reveals, there was much more conversation about the role of Partition than in others.

The contributions not only provide a valuable addition to the existing literature on Partition, but also hint at further avenues for research. More is still required, for example, on the extent to which the Punjab refugee experience was unique or reflective of developments beyond the region, especially concerning the refugee–state relationship and the trope of self-reliance.[14] With respect to the transmission of memories of Partition, further work could be done on the impact of collective on personal memory, and also on the ways in which the fluctuating Indo-Pakistan relationship has framed recollections. Finally, the imbalance between India-centric and Pakistan-centric accounts of Partition requires further exploration. The question could be raised as to whether lying beneath the obvious signs of divergence in these accounts there is evidence of a more subtle convergence.

NOTES

1. See I. Talbot and Gurharpal Singh, *The Partition of India* (Cambridge, 2009).
2. See Anita Inder Singh, *The Origins of the Partition of India, 1936–1947* (Delhi, 1987).
3. There is a vast literature on communalism. Some authors see it as the outcome of a deliberate British 'divide and rule' policy, while others link it with the unintentional consequences of modernization within the setting of the colonial state. For a sophisticated understanding of the emergence of communal identities, see Sandria Freitag, *Public Arenas and the Emergence of Communalism in North India* (Delhi, 1990).
4. See Lucy Chester, *On the Edge: Borders, Territory and Conflict in South Asia* (Manchester, 2008).
5. For a discussion of some of the earlier criticisms, see I. Talbot, 'The Mountbatten Viceroyalty Revisited: Themes and Controversies', in C.M. Woolgar (ed.), *Mountbatten on the Record* (Southampton, 1997), pp. 53–74. For the most recent criticism of Mountbatten's role, see S. Wolpert, *Shameful Flight: The Last Years of the British Empire in India* (New York: OUP, 2006).
6. For a discussion of the debates surrounding the number of casualties, see G. Pandey, *Remembering Partition: Violence, Nationalism and History in India* (Cambridge, 2001), p. 91.
7. The figures given for the number of refugees vary, as they do for the victims of Partition.

Migration continued in the Bengal area throughout the 1950s, and if this is added to the initial upheaval in the Punjab and other areas of North India, a figure of between 18 and 20 million migrants is arrived at.

8. See R.J. Moore, *Churchill, Cripps and India, 1939–1945* (Oxford, 1979); Anita Inder Singh, *The Origins of the Partition of India, 1936–1947* (Delhi, 1987); H.V. Hodson, *The Great Divide: Britain–India–Pakistan* (London, 1969).

9. For a recent Hindu nationalist interpretation of the events leading to Partition, see chapter 4 especially of L.K. Advani, *My Country, My Life* (New Delhi, 2008).

10. In addition to Wolpert's *Shameful Flight*, see Andrew Roberts, *Eminent Churchillians* (London, 1994).

11. Urvashi Butalia, *The Other Side of Silence: Voices from the Partition of India* (New Delhi, 1988); Ritu Menon and Kamla Bhasin, *Borders and Boundaries: Women in India's Partition* (New Delhi, 1988).

12. For a discussion of the criticisms, see Talbot and Singh, *The Partition of India*, p. 19.

13. Hasan pioneered the use of the Manto short story 'Toba Tek Singh' as a symbol of the confused identities arising from the upheaval of Partition. He later edited volumes on Partition which contained short stories as historical source material. Mushirul Hasan (ed.), *India's Partition: Process, Strategy and Mobilization* (New Delhi, 1994) and *India Partitioned: The Other Face of Freedom*, 2 vols (Delhi, 1995).

14. Joya Chatterji's work on Bengal provides scope for further reflections on the similarities and differences between the Punjab and Bengal refugee experience. These were rooted in timing and the patterns of migration in the two partitioned provinces and in the government resource allocations and attitudes to the 'refugee problem'. Joya Chatterji, 'Right or Charity? The Debate over Relief and Rehabilitation in West Bengal in 1947–50', in Suvir Kaul (ed.), *The Politics of Memory: The Aftermath of the Division of India* (New Delhi, 2001), pp. 74–111; *The Spoils of Partition: Bengal and India, 1947–1967* (Cambridge, 2007).

INHERITED MEMORIES

SECOND-GENERATION PARTITION NARRATIVES FROM PUNJABI FAMILIES IN DELHI AND LAHORE

Vanita Sharma
St Antony's College, Oxford University

ABSTRACT   This article explores the creation and transmission of second generation memories concerning the 1947 Partition of British India. The research is based on oral interviews with Punjabi families who migrated because of Partition and now live in Lahore and Delhi. It explores how Partition memories have been transmitted across generations within these families, and also examines similarities and differences between how the second generation interviewees from Delhi and Lahore remember Partition. It demonstrates that the second generation have not passively accepted everything that the first generation, or the state, has told them about Partition. The second generation's memories are also shaped by their age, nationality, religion and class, and the nature of contemporary politics.

Keywords: Partition, Pakistan, Delhi, Lahore, second generation, memory

INTRODUCTION

When British colonial rule in India came to an end in 1947, the subcontinent was partitioned to create two new sovereign states: India and Pakistan. The new international boundary was demarcated primarily on the basis of religion, with the majority Muslim provinces forming Pakistan and the majority non-Muslim provinces forming India. However, it was also decided that the Muslim-majority Punjab and Bengal would be internally partitioned, so that the non-Muslim areas of these provinces would remain in India.[1] The Partition triggered one of the largest mass migrations in modern history. Approximately 14.5 million people were displaced, with Hindus and Sikhs fleeing to India and Muslims fleeing to Pakistan. Furthermore, it is estimated that up to one million people were killed during communal rioting. The violence was at its most severe in the Punjab, which led to the migration of millions of Hindus and Sikhs from West Punjab and Muslims from East Punjab within the space of only a few months.

Until recently, however, the human consequences of Partition received very little scholarly attention. Historical research centred primarily on analysing the reasons why Partition occurred, and so mostly focused on an examination of the nature of pre-Partition politics.[2] It is only in the past two decades that the emphasis has now shifted,

Address for correspondence: Vanita Sharma, St Antony's College, 62 Woodstock Road, Oxford, OX2 6JF, UK. E-mail: vanitasha@gmail.com

Cultural and Social History, Volume 6, Issue 4, pp. 411–428 © The Social History Society 2009
DOI 10.2752/147800409X466254

and historians have begun to investigate the lived experience of Partition.[3] Utilizing a diverse range of source materials (ranging from official government records and memoirs to fictional literature and the oral history accounts of survivors), this new research has analysed the construction of the popular memory and experience of Partition, and has examined how gender, class, caste, religion and regional identities influenced the way that people were affected by Partition.

This article seeks to contribute to this new historiography of Partition, but it approaches the study of the popular memory in a different way. It focuses on the relationship between generation and memory. This issue has already received some attention within the field of Partition studies. Some scholars have concentrated on the role of generational identity in shaping the differential experiences of those who lived through Partition.[4] For instance, Urvashi Butalia has examined the distinctive ways in which children were affected by Partition.[5] Others have analysed the influences which have shaped the memories of the post-Partition generations. Scholars using this approach look primarily at how the Indian, Pakistani and Bangladeshi states have influenced the way that subsequent generations remember Partition through school history textbooks.[6] Krishna Kumar, for example, has examined how official Indian and Pakistani textbooks use divergent approaches to teach the history of Partition.[7] So far, however, scholarly research has focused mainly on the perceptions of present-day children and not on the older post-Partition generations. This article aims to redress this gap by examining the intergenerational transmission of memories about Partition within the family to the second generation, who are the children of those who lived through Partition.

This research does not, therefore, reveal any new empirical insights about what happened during Partition. Instead, its aim is to examine how Partition memories have been remembered and preserved within the family. It explores the transmission of memories across the generations, focusing specifically on how those who experienced Partition passed on their memories to the second generation. It also addresses the issue of how much similarity and difference there is between the Partition memories of the second generation interviewees from Delhi and Lahore. The two key questions that this article seeks to address are: how and why did the first generation pass on their memories of Partition, and why and to what degree have the second generation preserved these memories?

METHODOLOGY

The emergence of oral history has had an important role in changing the way that history is written and studied. It has enabled historians to explore the voices and experiences of people who were previously excluded or marginalized within the historical narrative. For these reasons, oral history research has been a valuable resource for the new Partition historiography which focuses on examining the popular memory of Partition.[8] However, like all forms of historical evidence, oral evidence has limitations which must be taken into account when it is used. Memory is changeable; oral accounts can change over time and oral testimonies vary considerably according to who the interviewer is and how the interview is conducted. Furthermore, another problem with oral evidence is that it is difficult to ascertain whether an interviewee's account is factually accurate, biased or exaggerated. The reliability of oral testimonies can also be questioned because the passage of time and present day events inevitably have an impact on how and what we remember. To counterbalance these vulnerabilities of oral history, historians who use oral evidence often stress that they have employed it as one of many sources, relying also on traditional written source materials to provide background and contextual research which verifies and expands on the evidence provided by the oral interviews. Most Partition scholars, for example, have used oral history as a complementary source together with more traditional textual sources in order to study the human experience of Partition.[9]

Although a variety of textual sources for background and contextual research have been utilized for this study, it relies primarily on oral interviews. It takes a different approach to interpreting oral evidence, however. It follows the approach of oral historians who acknowledge that we cannot be completely sure of the reliability of the testimonies that we collate, but who regard the subjectivity of oral history as a benefit not a flaw. This new approach to oral history has thus shifted from simply regarding oral history as a source of eyewitness accounts which can provide insights about the past which are missed in conventional historical records, to instead regarding it as being a valuable source with which to examine how memories are constructed and used.[10] Alessandro Portelli, for instance, has argued that 'even when [oral sources] do not tell the events as they occurred, the discrepancies and the errors are themselves events, clues for the work of desire and pain over time, for the painful search for meaning'.[11] This approach to using oral evidence is particularly appropriate for the study of family memories. For, as Elizabeth Stone has argued: 'When it comes to family stories, everything depends more on the uses made of them than on their content alone.'[12]

There is considerable methodological variety in generational research, and generation can be used in a variety of ways as an analytical concept.[13] This article applies the label of generation within the context of kinship. It defines the first generation as being those members of the family who lived through, and have first-hand memories of, Partition. It applies the label of second generation to those who do not have direct memories of Partition, and who thus acquired memories about the family's Partition experiences from the first generation. The second generation interviewees in this study were born between 1943 and 1963. Those born between 1943 and 1947 were obviously alive during Partition, but have been included in the second generation category because their young age at the time meant that they did not have personal, first-hand memories of the event.

This research is based on 135 oral interviews conducted with the first and second generation members of Punjabi families from Delhi and Lahore who migrated to India and Pakistan because of Partition. It focuses on families from Delhi and Lahore because these two cities were the most popular urban destinations for Punjabi Partition refugees in India and Pakistan. However, it is important to note that these case studies cannot be taken as representative of all Partition refugees in India and Pakistan. Instead, this study offers conclusions which pertain specifically to these families. Furthermore, restrictions of space mean that only a few of these interviewees' stories will be examined in this article. The interviews were conducted between 2003 and 2004, using semi-structured questions in order to achieve a balance between encouraging the interviewees to talk and direct the interview as much as possible and also ensuring that the same broad themes and issues were covered with each person. The interviewees were asked to narrate whatever stories or anecdotes they remembered about how and why their families migrated, and were also asked about how their families rebuilt their lives after Partition. Finally, the interviewees were asked their opinions on why Partition happened.

The interviewees have all been given pseudonyms, as some wished to have anonymity. The interviews were conducted in a variety of settings, with some people interviewed individually and others in groups. The families came from a broad range of socio-economic backgrounds and their experiences during Partition also varied significantly. All of the families that were interviewed currently live in Delhi and Lahore, but they arrived in these cities at different times. Some of the families migrated directly to these cities, but other families initially settled elsewhere and went to Delhi and Lahore weeks, months and, in some cases, even years later. Whilst some were able to migrate without encountering any danger, others lost family members during the communal violence; and whilst some families were able to preserve their assets, others arrived penniless.

Finally, it is important to bear in mind the specific context in which these oral testimonies were collated. The interviews were conducted between 2003 and 2004 and thus coincided with the initiation of the Indo-Pak peace process, during which period the borders were softened, transport networks were re-established, cricket diplomacy matches occurred, and the mutual ban on travel visas ended. As will be seen in the following section, this context had an important influence on the narratives given by the second generation.

The quality of the narratives collated also depended greatly on my being able to build up trust and rapport with the interviewees. For instance, in both India and Pakistan some interviews were cancelled or refused, because respondents feared I may be a spy for the Indian government or for the West. The identity of the interviewer can have an important influence on how open the interviewee is. The type of memories that interviewees are willing to share can vary considerably depending on whether the interviewer is regarded as an insider or outsider to the family and/or community.[14] I belong to an Indian Punjabi family, and my paternal grandfather was originally from the West Punjab, which is now in Pakistan. Questions about my own roots were frequently raised in the interviews, and sometimes my background helped me build a connection and trust with my interviewees from both Delhi and Lahore – like them, I was Punjabi, I had ancestral roots in Pakistan, and my family were also affected by Partition. However, I was also very much an outsider in both countries, as I was born and live in England, and there was also a generation gap with my interviewees, because I am part of the third generation. These interviews provide valuable evidence with which to study the process of how memories were transmitted between the first and second generations. However, it is important to note that these interviews are the product of a dialogue with an interviewer who was an outsider to the family. Thus, they specifically reveal how members of the second generation were willing to share or not share their private family memories in public.

THE TRANSMISSION OF PARTITION MEMORIES WITHIN THE FAMILY

Not all of the first-generation witnesses to Partition chose to discuss their experiences and memories with their children. For some Partition refugees their experiences were too traumatic for them to want to remember. Several potential interviewees from the second generation declined to be interviewed, insisting that their parents had never really spoken to them about that time. They explained that the first generation had not wanted to talk about it, because their parents had believed that Partition was best forgotten altogether. In these families the first generation had simply not considered it necessary or appropriate to talk about and pass on these memories to the second generation. Furthermore, not all in the second generation were necessarily interested in listening to these stories. The importance of the remembrance and preservation of these memories was therefore not something all families agreed upon. For some families, forgetting the Partition was much more important than remembering it. The interviews being explored in this article are therefore only representative of those families where Partition memories were actively passed down across the generations. These are families where the first generation found that remembrance, rather than suppression, of their Partition memories was more effective in helping them come to terms with the upheavals and traumas that they had experienced. However, even within these families, the second generation attached varying degrees of significance to these Partition stories.

From the families who were interviewed, the vast majority of the second generation respondents said that they recalled hearing stories about the Partition from their family members whilst they were growing up. However, the extent to which the first generation spoke about their memories with their children varied considerably, which meant that the second generation interviewees from Delhi and Lahore had different levels of knowledge about their family's experiences. Some families went into considerable depth and spoke frequently and openly about their memories, whereas others were much more restrained and did not speak about Partition very often, or so expansively. For instance, when asked about whether his parents had told him many stories about Partition, Harjinder (Sikh male), a retired cable manufacturer from Delhi, explained: 'They didn't tell us many stories, and we didn't often ask them to talk to us about Partition either.'[15] Harjinder's knowledge of his family's Partition experiences was thus, unsurprisingly, not very detailed. Over time, there were also differences in how frequently families talked about Partition. In some families they began to speak less about Partition as the years went by. For instance, Kirpal (Sikh male), a grocery shop owner from Delhi, said of his parents: 'They did tell us a lot about their experiences, as you do when things are new, but as time goes by you stop talking about it.'[16]

The way that these memories were passed on to the second generation also differed. The transmission of stories from the first generation to the second generation did not always occur between parents and children. In some cases, the second generation heard stories from other relatives, such as grandparents or aunts and uncles. For example, Balraj (Hindu male), a tailor from Delhi, recalled:

> My father didn't tell me [about Partition], my mother did. And one of my aunts, who was a widow, she told us. When it was night and I would go to sleep, I would hear the stories. I really enjoyed listening to stories of their lives, how they lived, how they came here, etc.[17]

Some second generation interviewees only learned of these stories indirectly, when they sat with the family whilst the adults talked about their memories among themselves. In other cases, where families did not talk about Partition, the second generation sometimes still heard first-hand accounts from other sources in the community, such as from their teachers or neighbours.

The first generation's re-telling of stories about Partition could serve different functions – and very often their class background appeared to have an important role in determining the type of memories that they chose to share with the second generation. Family memories did not always only focus on the trauma caused by Partition. Balraj, for instance, recalled that he had been told that his family were 'well settled and middle class' and were reasonably well off before Partition, with 'plenty of food and drink'.[18] Balraj took pride in these nostalgic memories about the prosperous and more relaxed life that his family had before Partition. He enjoyed hearing these stories, as they indicated that his family had a good social standing.

In other families, sharing memories about Partition was primarily a means through which the first generation could express their grief about the losses and tragedies they had suffered. For example, Nadir (Muslim male), a university professor from Lahore, recalled how his grandmother used to tell her grandchildren stories about Partition when they were young: 'When we were small children, five years old, she used to call us to come and sit down and listen to the stories of how we came here. She would be crying as she made "bread" [*roti*].'[19] However, whilst Nadir was able to empathize with his grandmother's grief, other second generation interviewees found this much harder to do. For example, Jaspreet (Sikh female), a schoolteacher from Delhi, said that her father found it impossible to forget his old home and still continued to reminisce about it today. She explained:

> Oh, every time they used to talk about it! Every time! Every time! When my father comes here it is the same topic – Pakistan, Pakistan, and nothing else! He would just go on and on about how they used to live there, they used to do that, everything![20]

She could sympathize with how traumatic it must have been for him to lose his home. However, she became uncomfortable when these memories and lingering feelings of attachment unsettled and conflicted with her ideas about national identity and loyalty. She found it impossible to accept that her father still identified his home as being in Pakistan. Jaspreet said:

> It is difficult to leave the house and leave everything and … go to a new place. Even today my father says, 'Oh, my house!', and my daughter the other day said, 'Why your house? You have lived in Delhi for many more years of your life. Why do you say "your house"? Your house is in Delhi. Why do you say "my house in Pakistan"'?[21]

Like her daughter, Jaspreet could not identify with or accept her father's feelings of homesickness because she considered Delhi to be her 'home'. Moreover, she felt that nearly sixty years after Partition, her father should feel the same way as her. The fact that she and her father defined 'home' differently frustrated her.

Although Jaspreet's tone in relating these anecdotes was jovial, it still hinted at her underlying unease. Her choice of vocabulary highlighted the source of the tension. Jaspreet defined the family's 'home' as being in Delhi. However, she emphasized that, by contrast, her father defined his 'home' as being in Pakistan. Whilst Jaspreet defined her 'home' by locality, she repeatedly described his 'home' in a national sense – as being in Pakistan rather than in Rawalpindi. She thereby emphasized that the source of tension between them rested on the issue of nationalist loyalties. Whilst she could sympathize with her father's nostalgia for his childhood home, she was irritated by the fact that he longed for a 'home' that was not only outside India but in Pakistan – perceived by many Indians as an enemy. His comments about his sense of belonging to what could be perceived as an alien homeland irked her because she felt the family belonged to India. Her father's attachment to his old house transcended the issue of national boundaries, but Jaspreet could not ignore this factor.

One of the key reasons for Jaspreet's sense of unease was the nature of post-Partition relations between India and Pakistan. The second generation grew up against the backdrop of prolonged and ongoing conflict between India and Pakistan. The continuing mistrust and enmity between the two countries made it difficult for the second generation to share the first generation's nostalgic longing for the homes that they had left behind. The second generation was much more emotionally detached and distanced from the first generation's nostalgic memories about their family's former homes. Although the second generation could empathize with the sense of pain and loss that the first generation felt as a consequence of being uprooted from their homes, many of them found it hard to identify with the yearning that the first generation continued to feel for these homes. As in Jaspreet's case, nostalgic memories which highlighted the first generation's lingering emotional ties to their former homes often made the second generation uncomfortable, as they did not share this personal attachment. In particular, they often found it could be hard to come to terms with the first generation's feelings of belonging to a place that was situated within a country to which they felt no nationalist allegiance – and, in some cases, regarded as their enemy.

However, another reason that Jaspreet believed that Partition should be forgotten was because the relationship between India and Pakistan appeared to be improving. Although Jaspreet was knowledgeable about her parents' experiences and said that she had found it interesting to hear about the 'tough time' that people had gone through during Partition, she personally felt it would be better to just forget that time.[22] She explained: 'Now it should be forgotten. I feel the new generation is not going to accept it or like it.'[23] Jaspreet strongly felt that it was detrimental for future generations to hold on to these bitter memories and argued that, in the context of improving relations between India and Pakistan, Partition should be forgotten. Jaspreet's comments were thus clearly influenced by the timing of the interview, which took place during the 2004 cricket diplomacy tournament between India and Pakistan, when much media attention was focused on promoting reconciliation between Indians and Pakistanis at the popular level. She argued that, for there to be peace between the two countries, future generations needed to leave the memories of Partition behind.

Some second generation interviewees found it much easier to share the first generation's grief and nostalgia where these stories served to emphasize the elevated social status of the family. For example, Rajan (Hindu male), a print shop owner from Delhi, recounted how his mother cried every night when she remembered what had happened to their family. He said:

> there was no 'bread' (*roti*) for us to eat, just one small bowl of the vegetable and that was it. She would say, 'Eat this and go to bed. There is nothing more.' Over there we were millionaires and here we had to eat one small bowl of vegetables and go to sleep – we suffered so much … She sobbed throughout whilst narrating this story.[24]

It is evident that Rajan's mother's grief lingered for many years, caused not just by the experiences the family had gone through during Partition but also by the negative impact it continued to have on her family life afterwards, especially the fall in their standard of living. Rajan described with empathy the pain that his mother went through, as she felt both despair and frustration at being unable to provide her children with sufficient food or clothing. The family's circumstances had been significantly reduced compared to their wealthy status prior to Partition. In this context, for Rajan's mother, the sharing of these memories with her son served as both an apology and an explanation to him about why the family was in this situation. His father had gone from being a successful gold wholesale trader, who owned his own business selling gold to jewellers for manufacturing, to being unemployed with not enough money to provide his family with the basic amenities of life. It was only much later that Rajan's father found a job again, this time as a gold commission agent.

By telling Rajan stories of his family's experiences during Partition, his mother was therefore able to explain to him the reasons for their impoverishment and her subsequent helplessness at being unable to give him as much as she could have before. These stories about how his family had been well established and wealthy, owning a successful gold business for seven generations, also enabled Rajan's mother to instil in him a sense of family pride and identity. All other markers of his ancestry – their wealth, their home, their business and the social recognition of the family in the community – were now gone. In contrast to Jaspreet, Rajan had no apprehensions about talking about his mother's regretful memories. Rajan was comfortable in relating these stories about his family's earlier wealth, because in doing so he illustrated that his family's status was more elevated than his current social standing indicated.

In other families, the stories that were passed on by the first generation were not necessarily focused on regret. For example, Imran (Muslim male), a medical doctor from Lahore, said that his family had also frequently spoken about Partition and about the more prosperous lives that the family had had beforehand.[25] Like Nadir and Rajan, he also enjoyed hearing these stories during his childhood. He explained: 'Partition was often talked about in our childhood days – there was nostalgia about places we had lived in for centuries and the more privileged life that they had.'[26] As in the case of Rajan, his parents were also trying to pass on to him a sense of the family's ancestral history. However, the context that Imran's parents placed these stories in was very different. Both Nadir and Rajan were told stories that were about regret, highlighting the pain and hardship that the family had been forced to go through as a result of Partition. Like Rajan's mother, Imran's parents told him stories about the family's lost wealth. However, Imran's family memorialized their loss within a different framework. His family voluntarily migrated to Pakistan, and so were not refugees. Imran explained that his parents had been supportive of the creation of Pakistan, because they believed in pan-Islamism. Imran situated the creation of Pakistan within the context of how Muslim identity had been progressively diminished during the colonial period and afterwards, continuing to the present day. He explained:

> Their [Western] dukes, barons and countries are given a larger-than-life picture. Our own aristocrats are reduced to footmen – they degraded the aristocrats of the subcontinent, the Muslim subcontinent. The aristocratic dress was given to footmen, guards and sepoys. Turkish caps were put on monkeys – it was all pre-planned. This is how Muslim civilisation was being deliberately degraded and is still being degraded – the glory of Muslims was being watered down, to make sure that they would not be inspired again.[27]

Imran thus regarded the losses that his family endured because of Partition as symbolic of the personal contribution they had made in support of a wider pan-Islamic cause to help rebuild and recover lost Muslim cultural and religious pride. Imran therefore re-told the stories of what his family had lost through Partition with pride for a different reason. He was proud of the sacrifices that his family had made for the creation of Pakistan.

However, whilst the second generation interviewees often disagreed over how and why these stories were significant to the present, one thing that most of them had in common was the emphasis they gave to the differences between their narratives and those of the first generation, stressing that it was their parents who had experienced the reality of the Partition. As Jaspreet explained:

> Yes, we were really interested to hear them talk about Partition. But these were really [just] stories for us because we had not seen it or observed [the Partition ourselves].[28]

When compared to the stories told by the first generation, it was evident that many of the second generation interviewees were able to give detailed knowledge about their families' experiences of Partition and often narrated these stories with considerable accuracy. Nevertheless, the second generation interviewees were deeply sensitive to the fact that they were not first-hand witnesses and consistently emphasized that their knowledge was secondary. Although perhaps an obvious point, this was of considerable importance to the second generation interviewees. They frequently stressed this distinction during their interviews, in order to emphasize the validity and authenticity of the stories they narrated. This sometimes made the second generation interviewees reluctant to talk about what they recalled, especially if their elders were still alive. Some of the second generation interviewees therefore questioned the historical value of their own secondary narratives – and, in some cases, the historical value of this research.

As well as there being different levels of willingness within the second generation to talk about Partition, from amongst those who did choose to remember there were also divisions over whether this process of remembrance was worthwhile. The second generation's opinions about the contemporary relevance of these stories were clearly important regarding whether they felt that these memories were worth preserving or not. Some interviewees explained that whilst these stories may have given them a sense of their family background and identity, they felt that the relevance of Partition stories to the present was minimal. Harjinder (male, Sikh), for example, questioned whether there was any need to remember: 'these are just [better] left as stories. Is there any point in repeating them?'[29] Saleem (male, Muslim), a property dealer from Lahore, agreed. He explained: 'I am uneducated so I don't know about Partition. I had no time to ask about Partition. I didn't think about it.'[30] He argued: 'Why are you so obsessed about the past? It is over now. Those who died, died so let it go. Be concerned about now. The dead died with their stories. We are not concerned. What use is it? I am concerned about getting money and providing for my family.'[31] Saleem felt that, within the context of the daily struggle to survive, stories about Partition were irrelevant.

Other second generation interviewees expressed a reluctance to talk about certain aspects of their families' Partition memories. For example, Navpreet (Sikh female), the co-manager of a small grocery shop in Delhi, explained that whilst she remembered hearing these tales, she did not identify with them and was consequently disinterested.[32] Navpreet believed Partition was over and so felt that all that should be remembered was that it should not happen again:

> Look, those people who saw Partition with their own eyes, they are the ones who understand what happened. They think about what happened. What is there for us to think about? What can we think about? Those people to whom it happened, they remember. For me it is just a story. All I think is this kind of thing should not happen but it is finished and I do not take a lot of interest in it.[33]

However, her comments must be understood within context. They arose as an attempt to silence her husband's discussion of sexual violence during Partition, which she felt was a taboo subject. Her husband, Gurdas, co-managed the grocery store with her and was a first generation interviewee, who was aged fourteen in 1947.[34] Navpreet felt that it was inappropriate for him to discuss Partition with a young woman (me) and became particularly agitated when he began talking about violence against women:

> Gurdas: There were people who dishonoured girls. If there were good-looking girls, they would make them naked and they would take out a parade of them – the Muslims. They would make them sit with them naked and smoke hookah.
> Navpreet: Don't tell her these things!

Gurdas: Meaning these things happened. Meaning young girls they would make them sit naked and say 'Hey, you come over here!' … Some days they would cut them up – especially those girls who came from prominent families. This type of thing happened.

Navpreet: Stop this talk![35]

Navpreet's reluctance to discuss this topic was not simply because she felt that it was best forgotten or that it was socially inappropriate. It became clear within the course of the interview that she was also very nervous about the fact that the interview was being taped, and about whether I was potentially working for the government. She was worried about whether anything that they were saying could be held against them, and was concerned to make sure that her husband was not saying anything controversial. Although she said that she felt that Partition violence was best forgotten, she was clearly anxious that these memories could be potentially politically sensitive.

For other second generation interviewees, the scale and form of violence that occurred during Partition was precisely the reason why they felt that it needed to be remembered. Kuldeep (Sikh female), a teacher from Delhi, for example, attributed great importance to my hearing her family's Partition stories about violence against women.[36] Prior to the formal interview that I conducted with her, we spoke informally and she narrated to me at length the experiences of her family during Partition. She was very familiar with these stories and could narrate them in considerable detail. However, during our formal recorded interview, she was reluctant to talk and was keen for me to talk instead to her older sister and sister-in-law, both of whom had first-hand memories of that time. She did not feel comfortable speaking in place of them, as they were still alive and able to give their own testimonies. Nevertheless, she emphasized that she attributed great importance to these memories. Kuldeep's personal experiences of the impact of communal violence during the 1984 anti-Sikh riots had reinforced for her the need to remember Partition. Unable to forget her traumatic experiences in 1984 when she saw her house set on fire by rioters with her husband and son still inside, she had gained a greater appreciation for how the elder generation of her family also could not forget what had happened to them during Partition. Kuldeep believed that the horrors that families like hers had suffered as a result of the communal violence during Partition and 1984 alike should not be forgotten, because her own experiences highlighted the fact that communal violence continued to be a problem in society.

The second generation interviewees were therefore divided over how they related to these Partition stories. Some, like Kuldeep, shared the emotional investment of the first generation for whom the grief, trauma and losses of Partition were still real, whereas others, such as Navpreet, were more distanced and regarded these memories as being too controversial; still others, like Saleem, believed that Partition memories were now simply irrelevant. Thus, one of the core factors which determined the second generation's attitudes towards whether Partition was worth remembering or not was their view about its relevance to present day issues.

The improved political climate between India and Pakistan meant that some interviewees had also begun to question the accuracy of the narratives that their families had passed down to them. Amna (Muslim female), a housewife from Lahore, described how her feelings towards Indians had now changed.[37] She grew up hearing stories about the horrors of Partition from her mother, who had fled to Pakistan from Nabha in East Punjab. She explained:

> When I was young, I was more impressed [by these Partition stories]. I used to hear these things with more interest. Now I have grown more mature, more realistic. Maybe, because of … age … Now I am more realistic. I think people can be bad anywhere. Bad and good. This is not the criterion that he is Indian so he is bad, and this person is Pakistani and therefore he is good.[38]

However, it was not simply her age that had made Amna begin to question the narrative imbibed as a child. She had been forced to start re-thinking her views through encouragement from her sons, who were living abroad and had made Indian friends. Her own experience of making Indian friends when she lived in London for five years also led her to begin questioning her perceptions. She explained:

> When I lived in England I had an Indian friend and she was good. I had an English friend and she was very friendly. She was a good natured person. The same is with my sons. They had some very good natured Indian friends. So things have changed.[39]

These experiences made her question whether the stereotypes she had formed (from the Partition stories that she had heard) were still applicable to contemporary Indian and Pakistani society. More recently, she explained, she had begun to question whether even the narrative she had been taught about Partition was completely accurate, following the shift in media depictions of India after the initiation of the peace process. She explained:

> We were taught Partition was very important as Muslims and Hindus cannot live together. I don't know about this, because I didn't see it. But it has been instilled in us that we wouldn't have a life like this if we were in India. We try to do the same with our kids telling them that Pakistan is very important. Indians are the enemy. I don't know if it is true. We have been told again and again that we couldn't live together … Now we are hearing things about human rights and delegations – now we are hearing that we should be more friendly [rather than enemies], but throughout this period I heard that we couldn't live together, that Muslims were not given enough jobs. That is what we have heard from different sources.[40]

She explained that all she had learned from her family and from school and from articles in the newspapers and magazines had reinforced these views, but now she was beginning to revise her opinions.

Recent media stories about Partition thus appeared to have quite an important role in leading the second generation to question their earlier opinions about Partition. For example, Bilal (Muslim male), a senior manager in a government-owned utilities company in Lahore, credited the media with creating an awareness of the different interpretations about why Partition had happened, which meant that people now had a better understanding of how Indians interpreted the causes of Partition differently from Pakistanis.[41] He said: 'I think the minds of the people have been changed, because the media, television, etc. has a big role.'[42]

However, whilst several of the second generation interviewees explained that they now had an increased awareness and understanding of the different opinions expressed in the other country, this did not always mean that they had changed their views about Partition. Some interviewees challenged and resisted the way in which the opposing nationalistic interpretations of Partition were being questioned. For example, Noreen, a housewife from Lahore, observed: 'The government has pushed this thing out, that we should get on.'[43] She recalled the positive experiences that her family had when they met a writer who was visiting from India. She explained:

> He was so loving. We had dinner together. His face resembled my father's. My brother later went to hear him at a conference three or four years later. He contacted him and he [the writer] said take a taxi and stay here with me and bring your wife and kids. It meant a lot that he said that. Then a few years later he came to Pakistan again and stayed with my brother.[44]

Regardless of the new bonds that had been built between these two families, Noreen stressed her opinion that the need for Pakistan, and the importance of Partition, were not diminished. The contemporary political climate influenced her opinions, but in a different way. She argued:

> Look at Palestine, Afghanistan, Kashmir. Jews, Christians, Hindus have been suppressing Muslims for centuries. It has been going on for centuries and it is a global conspiracy. It is not unique to India. Non-Muslims have an agenda to suppress the Muslims. Then they did it with simple technologies – now it is done with more complicated ones, like the War on Terror.[45]

Noreen felt that the suppression of Muslims was both a historic and a contemporary reality, and that both the past and the present demonstrated why Partition and the creation of Pakistan were so vital. She believed that Partition could not be forgotten, because it was not simply a story about the division of territory. It was about the foundation of a new country which had provided security and protection for the subcontinent's Muslims after the end of colonialism, which was something that she felt was still needed in the current global climate. For her, forgetting Partition was therefore impossible, because the memory of Partition and the creation of Pakistan were inseparable. Interviewees like Noreen showed that whilst communal stereotypes could be challenged on the individual level, mistrust remained on a collective level.

The creation of second generation memory is an active not a passive process. The second generation did not passively accept everything that the first generation, or the state, told them about Partition. Many of the interviewees showed that they had considered and questioned aspects of both their family and official memory. The expression of Partition memory, for both the first and second generations, was not static – their memories, attitudes and assumptions changed over time. Post-Partition and contemporary events were important factors in determining the contours of both first and second generation memory. Specific historical moments, such as the 1984 anti-Sikh riots in Delhi and the Indo-Pak peace process initiated in 2003, caused the second generation to reassess and question the memories that they had inherited from their parents – leading some to reject their parents' stories and others to endorse them.

CONCLUSIONS

This article has examined the creation and transmission of memory about Partition within families from Lahore and Delhi. The conclusions drawn from these cases studies cannot be regarded as being representative of all Partition refugee families in India and Pakistan, nor even as representative of all families who migrated to Lahore and Delhi. This research provides an insight into the construction of second generation memory, but these conclusions are specific to the individual families that were interviewed. However, as long as these limitations are borne in mind, some tentative conclusions can be made about some of the core generalities of second generation memory.

This research has shown that neither first nor second generation memory was homogeneous. These families from Delhi and Lahore were confronted by similar challenges in dealing with their Partition memories. The first generation dealt with the trauma of dislocation in different ways. Some found that reminiscing about the past with their children served as an important coping mechanism to deal with their sense of loss, and some passed on memories in order to give their children a sense of their family history and identity. However, in other families the first generation found their memories too traumatic to share and did not speak about them. In addition to the differences that emerged between the interviewees from Lahore and Delhi, contestation could also occur within generations too. Other group identities like class, religion and nationality, and the nature of contemporary politics, had a strong influence in shaping first and second generation Partition memories.

The way that the second generation responded to Partition stories also varied over time. As children, they recalled how these stories of bravery, courage, horror and danger held great fascination for them. As adults, the second generation interviewees had often reassessed their feelings about these stories and were more divided over the contemporary relevance of the stories, both for themselves personally and for society in general. Many of the second generation interviewees expressed a sense of unease over how these stories revealed that their ancestral roots lay in the 'other' country, whilst others remained unperturbed by this and remained curious about their origins. Some now questioned the partisan nature of accounts that had been passed down to them, whereas others steadfastly continued to believe in the veracity of their family stories. Furthermore, whilst some argued that the story of Partition continued to offer lessons and insights that were still relevant for society today, others argued that it was time to leave the memories behind and to forget Partition. As adults, the views of the second generation about their inherited Partition memories were shaped not just by what they had been told by the first generation, but also by their own views about the current political and social climate.

However, the question remains as to why historians should be concerned with the memories of a generation who did not experience Partition first hand? Research on post-memory is important because it demonstrates how historical events, such as

Partition, can continue to influence the identity and perceptions of subsequent generations, and it shows how historical memory, whilst being preserved through intergenerational transmission, can also change through this process.[46] This article has shown that there is considerable scope for more scholarly research on the intergenerational transmission of memory, and the formation of second generation memory in particular. For example, it would be useful to compare these oral narratives with those of the second generation from other groups, such as rural Punjabi migrants, Partition migrants from other regions of India, Pakistan and Bangladesh, and families who have subsequently emigrated outside of South Asia. In particular, it would be interesting to conduct further research on the second generation from those Partition refugee populations that have not assimilated as well as the Punjabis in India and Pakistan did. For instance, the second generation from families of Bengali refugees who migrated to India, Urdu-speaking Muhajirs in Sind and Bihari refugees in Bangladesh would probably have produced quite different testimonies.

This research on second generation Partition memories also allows for some tentative conclusions to be made about the similarities and differences between the second generation of Partition and Holocaust survivor families. In academic research, there has been much greater recognition of the long-term psychological impact of the Holocaust on the second generation.[47] Eva Hoffman, for example, has described the second generation in Holocaust survivor families as being a 'hinge generation': she explained that members of this generation are simultaneously distant from and close to the Holocaust, because they did not experience it first hand but have a 'living connection' to those who did.[48] Consequently the second generation, she argued, is the generation which initiates the process of coming to terms with, and making sense of, Holocaust memory. However, Hoffman explained that this was a process which evolved over time, with the second generation progressing through different 'stages of understanding' throughout their lifetime.[49] The way that they understood and related to the Holocaust changed as they aged and progressed through different stages in the life cycle, but also as society's views about remembering the Holocaust changed through the decades. This article has shown that a similar process can be delineated in the experiences of the second generation interviewees from Lahore and Delhi, as the way that they related to their family's Partition memories also varied with age. As adults, the second generation from these families did not simply echo what they had been taught by their families, the state and society. Their narratives were more reflective; the second generation questioned the accuracy of what they had been told as children and also reconsidered the relevance that these stories had today.

The political context surrounding the memory of traumatic events also has an important influence on how and whether family memory will be preserved by the second generation. Resistance to and ambivalence about family origins is something that the second generation from Holocaust survivor families have in common with the second generation from Partition survivor families. However, the second generation in Holocaust survivor families are often posited as being 'memory-bearers' who have responsibility for preserving the first generation's Holocaust memories after they have died.[50] Memory preservation in the second generation of Jewish Holocaust survivors has been much more formalized and institutionalized because remembering the Holocaust has a greater international and political significance. Preserving Holocaust survivors' individual stories forms part of the Jewish community's efforts to ensure that the events of the Holocaust are never forgotten or the truth of it denied. The preservation of family stories of the Holocaust by the second generation thus assumes a broader importance, because Holocaust memory has a central role in defining Jewish identity and in justifying the need for, and existence of, Israel.[51]

In contrast, the creation and transmission of Partition memories are situated within a very different political context. The story of Partition is central to how national identity is defined in both India and Pakistan, and Partition has had a defining influence on shaping the history and fortunes of these families. Nevertheless, the second generation interviewees from Delhi and Lahore expressed little interest in how Partition had collectively affected them as a generation. This is probably because, unlike the second generation in Holocaust survivor families, the second generation in the families of Partition survivors are not regarded by their wider community, or even by themselves, as having a formal role in preserving the memory of Partition. Instead, second generation interviewees from Lahore and Delhi frequently argued that this was not "their" story, it was their parents' story, and several suggested that the memory of Partition no longer had any relevance and was not worth talking about.

However, it is also important to recognize that the political context surrounding the construction of second generation memory about Partition is not fixed and static. It is thus worth noting again that this research was undertaken in 2003 and 2004, when a peace process had been initiated between India and Pakistan and both governments were advocating reconciliation between their people. Many of the interviewees' comments were clearly influenced by the changed political relationship between India and Pakistan and made direct references to how it had led them to reconsider the value and significance of the Partition memories that the first generation had passed down to them. However, in 2009, when this article was being written, there is renewed tension between India and Pakistan following the November 2008 terrorist attacks in Mumbai. If the interviews were conducted again in this new and more hostile political climate, it is questionable whether Navpreet from Delhi would still argue that 'it is finished and I do not take a lot of interest in it',[52] and whether Amna from Lahore would still argue that: 'This is not the criterion that he is Indian so he is bad, and this person is Pakistani and therefore he is good.'[53]

NOTES

1. For more information on how the boundary was demarcated, see Ishtiaq Ahmed, 'The 1947 Partition of Punjab: Arguments Put Forth before the Punjab Boundary Commission by the Parties Involved', and Joya Chatterji, 'The Making of a Borderline: The Radcliffe Award for Bengal', in Ian Talbot and Gurharpal Singh (eds), *Region and Partition: Bengal, Punjab and the Partition of the Subcontinent* (Karachi, 1999); and Lucy Chester, 'The 1947 Partition: Drawing the Indo-Pakistani Boundary', *American Diplomacy*, 7 (2002), http://www.unc.edu/depts/diplomat/archives_roll/2002_01-03/chester_partition/chester_partition.html#Anchor_top (accessed 1 June 2008).

2. See, for example, H.V. Hodson, *The Great Divide: Britain–India–Pakistan* (London, 1969); V.P. Menon, *The Transfer of Power in India* (London, 1957); Ayesha Jalal, *The Sole Spokesman: Jinnah, the Muslim League and the Demand for Pakistan* (Cambridge, 1985); and Sucheta Mahajan, *Independence and Partition: The Erosion of Colonial Power in India* (London, 2000).

3. See, for example, Ritu Menon and Kamla Bhasin, *Borders and Boundaries: Women in India's Partition* (New Delhi, 1998); Urvashi Butalia, *The Other Side of Silence: Voices from India's Partition* (New Delhi, 1998); Mushiral Hasan (ed.), *Inventing Boundaries: Gender, Politics and the Partition of India* (Delhi, Oxford, 2000); Gyan Pandey, *Remembering Partition: Violence, Nationalism and History in India* (Cambridge, 2001); S. Settar and Indira B. Gupta (eds), *Pangs of Partition: The Human Dimension* (New Delhi, 1999); Ian Talbot, *Divided Cities: Partition and Its Aftermath in Lahore and Amritsar 1947–1957* (Karachi, 2006); Ravinder Kaur, *Since 1947: Partition Narratives among Punjabi Migrants of Delhi* (New Delhi, 2007); and Vazira Fazila-Yacoobali Zamindar, *The Long Partition and the Making of Modern South Asia: Refugees, Boundaries, Histories* (New York, 2007).

4. Butalia, *The Other Side of Silence*, ch. 6; Meghna Guha Thakurta, 'Uprooted and Divided', *Seminar*, 510 (2002), http://www.india-seminar.com/2002/510/510%20 meghna%20 guha%20thakurta.htm (accessed 1 June 2008).

5. Butalia, *The Other Side of Silence*, ch. 6.

6. K.K. Aziz, *The Murder of History* (Lahore, 2004); Krishna Kumar, *Prejudice and Pride: School Histories of the Freedom Struggle in India and Pakistan* (New Delhi, 2001); Nita Kumar, 'Children and the Partition', in Suvir Kaul (ed.), *The Partitions of Memory: The Afterlife of the Division of India* (Bloomington, IN, 2001); Yvette Claire Rosser, *Indoctrinating Minds: A Case Study of Bangladesh* (New Delhi, 2004); Yvette Claire Rosser, *Islamization of Pakistan Social Studies Textbooks* (New Delhi, 2001).

7. Kumar, *Prejudice and Pride*, chapters 3, 4 and 11.

8. See, for example, Menon and Bhasin, *Borders and Boundaries*; Butalia, *The Other Side of Silence*; Talbot, *Divided Cities*; Kaur, *Since 1947*; Zamindar, *The Long Partition and the Making of Modern South Asia*.

9. Menon and Bhasin, *Borders and Boundaries*, pp. 13–14; Butalia, *The Other Side of Silence*, p. 15; Talbot, *Divided Cities*, pp. xxii–xxiv; Kaur, *Since 1947*, pp. 36–7; Zamindar, *The Long Partition and the Making of Modern South Asia*, pp.12–16.

10. For oral historians who use this methodological approach, see for example the works of Alessandro Portelli, *The Death of Luigi Trastulli and Other Stories: Form and Meaning in Oral History* (Albany, NY, 1991); Alistair Thompson, *Anzac Memories: Living with the Legend* (Melbourne, Oxford, 1994); Luisa Passerini, translated by Lisa Erdberg, *Autobiography of a Generation: Italy, 1968* (London, Hanover, 1996).

11. Alessandro Portelli, *The Order Has Been Carried out: History, Memory and Meaning of a Nazi Massacre in Rome* (New York, 2003), p. 16.

12. Elizabeth Stone, *Black Sheep and Kissing Cousins: How Our Family Stories Shape Us* (New Jersey, 2004, originally published 1998), p. 59.

13. For an analysis of the various challenges involved with using generation as an analytical category, see Peter Loizos, '"Generations" in Forced Migration: Towards Greater Clarity', *Journal of Refugee Studies*, 20 (2007): 193–209.

14. For further discussion of this issue, see Akemi Kikumura, 'Family Life Histories: A Collaborative Venture', and Belinda Bozzoli, 'Interviewing the Women of Pokeng', in Robert Perks and Alistair Thompson, *The Oral History Reader* (London, New York, 1998).

15. Harjinder, born in 1945, interviewed August 2004.

16. Kirpal, born in 1955, interviewed August 2004.

17. Balraj, born in 1960, interviewed September 2004.
18. Ibid.
19. Nadir, born in 1948, interviewed December 2003.
20. Jaspreet, born in 1953, interviewed August 2004.
21. Ibid.
22. Ibid.
23. Ibid.
24. Rajan, born in 1949, interviewed September 2004.
25. Imran, born in 1949, interviewed September 2003.
26. Ibid.
27. Ibid.
28. Jaspreet, born in 1953, interviewed August 2004.
29. Harjinder, born in 1945, interviewed August 2004.
30. Saleem, born in 1957, interviewed September 2003.
31. Ibid.
32. Navpreet, born in 1943, interviewed September 2004.
33. Ibid.
34. Gurdas, born in 1933, interviewed September 2004.
35. Navpreet and Gurdas, interviewed September 2004.
36. Kuldeep, born in 1947, interviewed August 2004.
37. Amna, born in 1947, interviewed January 2004.
38. Ibid.
39. Ibid.
40. Ibid.
41. Bilal, born in 1946, interviewed February 2004.
42. Ibid.
43. Noreen, born in 1943, interviewed January 2004.
44. Ibid.
45. Ibid.
46. For a definition of post-memory, see Marianne Hirsch, *Family Frames: Photography, Narrative and Postmemory* (Cambridge, MA, and London, 1997), p. 22–3.
47. For research on the second generation in Holocaust survivor families, see, for example, Eva Hoffman, *After Such Knowledge: A Meditation on the Aftermath of the Holocaust* (London, 2004); Helen Epstein, *Children of the Holocaust: Conversations with Sons and Daughters of Survivors* (New York, 1979); Aaron Hass, *In the Shadow of the Holocaust: The Second-Generation* (Ithaca, NY, 1990); and Efraim Sicher, *Breaking Crystal: Writing and Memory after Auschwitz* (Urbana, Chicago, IL, 1998).
48. Eva Hoffman, *After Such Knowledge*, p. xv.
49. Eva Hoffman, *After Such Knowledge,* p. xiv.
50. For example, see Alan L. Berger, 'Bearing Witness: Second Generation Literature of the Shoah', *Modern Judaism*, 10 (1990), pp. 44–5.
51. For more on the construction of collective memory about the Holocaust, see, for example, Peter Novick, *The Holocaust and Collective Memory: The American Experience* (London, 2000), ch. 1.
52. Navpreet, born in 1943, interviewed September 2004.
53. Amna, born in 1947, interviewed January 2004.

DISTINCTIVE CITIZENSHIP

REFUGEES, SUBJECTS AND POST-COLONIAL STATE IN INDIA'S PARTITION

Ravinder Kaur
Roskilde University, Denmark

ABSTRACT   The refugee, in India's Partition history, appears as an enigmatic construct – part pitiful, part heroic, though mostly shorn of agency – representing the surface of the human tragedy of Partition. Yet this archetype masks the undercurrent of social distinctions that produced hierarchies of post-colonial citizenship within the mass of refugees. The core principle of the official resettlement policy was *self-rehabilitation*, that is, the ability to become a productive citizen of the new nation state without state intervention. Thus, the onus of performing a successful transition – from refugee to citizen – lay on the resourcefulness of the refugees rather than the state. This article traces the differing historical trajectories followed by 'state-dependent' and 'self-reliant' refugees in the making of modern citizenry in post-colonial India.

Keywords: refugees, citizens, post-colonial state, social class, Partition, India

INTRODUCTION

In the history of India's Partition, the 'refugee' is a central – almost mythical – figure without which the national histories of India and Pakistan can hardly be told. The processes of Partition become particularly palpable when narrated through the lives of ordinary people who experienced violence and homelessness in the course of the boundary making between the two states. Thus, the official narrative of Partition is built around an abstract notion of 'refugee experience' wherein the multitude of refugees is often articulated as a singular body with a common origin, trajectory and destiny. This archetypal refugee appears as an enigmatic construct – part pitiful, part heroic, though mostly shorn of agency – representing the surface of the human tragedy of Partition, even as it masks the tense undercurrents and distinctive state practices of resettlement.

Partition scholarship has very recently begun un-forming this construct to excavate the underlying differences. A study of Bengal refugees has shown how an authentic refugee type within the state discourse was fashioned after the Punjab experience of internecine violence and movement.[1] This frame seldom fitted the Bengal refugees, whose journeys were not always entwined with dramatic episodes of violence and who were, thus, discursively located outside the orbit of authentic 'refugee-ness'. Elsewhere

Address for correspondence: Department of Cross-Cultural and Regional Studies, University of Copenhagen, Leifsgade 33, 2300 Copenhagen S, Denmark. E-mail: rkaur@ruc.dk

Cultural and Social History, Volume 6, Issue 4, pp. 429–446 © The Social History Society 2009
DOI 10.2752/147800409X466272

I have shown the *affects* of social differences on state policies of resettlement and the ways in which refugees were segregated and isolated – untouchables from upper castes, single women from families, poor from rich – in accord with prevalent social norms.[2] The transit camps and permanent refugee housing colonies were hardly levelling spaces where differences of class, geography, caste and gender would disappear against the larger-than-life canvas of Partition. The obvious question then is: how did this landscape of social differences among the refugees translate into a modern citizenry of post-colonial India? And what forms of hierarchies or grades within the citizenry were affected through this production of difference? The intricate linkages between the categories of refugees and citizens, and the ways in which one un/easily morphs into the other, are yet to be fully explored vis-à-vis Partition history.

The central analytical premise is that the *making of* and *becoming* post-colonial citizen-subjects were linked to the refugees' ability to *self-rehabilitate* rather than depend on the state for survival and recognition. Self-rehabilitation, here, suggests a governmental technology, pursued by the Indian state, aimed at producing self-supporting citizens out of the mass of refugees. In a way, it symbolized state-ordained *rites de passage* of growing up – from child to adult – and taking responsibility for oneself rather than depending on the state. Clearly, refugees were seen as minors who were being pushed by the paternalistic state to become adult citizens. In policy terms, this meant becoming proper subjects befitting the nation without being a burden on the state. In practice, becoming proper subjects depended on one's successful deployment of social capital, that is, one's possession not only of financial resources but also of useful social networks and cultural distinctions.[3] An individual's success in setting up homes, businesses and gaining employment, then, became the success of state policies, whereas failure to be self-reliant was an individual failure that the state was not responsible for. One's ability to survive outside of refugee camps and state institutions was linked to one's prospects of becoming relevant and full-fledged citizens of the new nation. Thus, the emerging citizenry itself was shaped by the differing trajectories of movement and resettlement traced by the refugees.

The following is an account of Partition resettlement history from two perspectives – state-dependent and self-reliant refugees – and their different journeys from being refugees to citizens in the new nation state. The account is based on extensive fieldwork conducted over a six-year period in refugee resettlement colonies in Delhi.[4] It also relies upon a vast newspaper archive as well as a variety of official documents.

DISTINCTIVE CITIZENSHIP

The notion of citizenship within Partition historiography is largely considered as given, and an uncomplicated one at that. This is because in most cases the legal status of citizenship was automatically conferred upon 'displaced persons' in post-colonial India.[5] Thus, enquiries into the transformative processes – of refugees into citizens – have hardly been pushed beyond the legal-technical boundaries of citizenship where the rights and responsibilities of individuals are considered universal in relation to the nation state.[6] Such a narrow conceptualization of citizenship limits our understanding of the architecture of social differences upon which the modern Indian citizenry was based. In this article, citizenship is conceptualized as 'a set of self constituting practices in different settings of powers', where power itself is understood as a social technology that induces being made and self-making.[7] In other words, citizenship is seen as a constant work-in-progress, shaped and realized in everyday life through strategies that newcomers adopt to negotiate different governmental authorities, and the state practices that seek to classify and define displaced people; pressure on the newcomers to integrate and self-define underpins this overlapping space between refugees and citizens. Far from being a universal and unified category in post-Partition India, I argue, citizenship appears as a polymorphous field upon which the distinctions and hierarchies of new subjects were negotiated with the post-colonial state. This distinctive citizenship becomes particularly visible within the spectacular imaginary of 'refugee' – a discursive lens through which to view the simultaneous processes of *being made* and *becoming* citizens of post-colonial India. While the first process suggests a set of transformative state practices to resettle the displaced populations, the second suggests an active effort by the displaced people themselves to gain resources and status by appropriating and redirecting those state practices. In both instances, the state's interventions to resolve the 'refugee problem' were influential in shaping the new citizenry, even though it sometimes reified the old social distinctions and prejudices of, for example, class and caste.

Two related arguments that underpin the central idea concern the identity and imaginary of 'refugee' that both state and migrants sought to define and appropriate. First, the label 'refugee' accrued moral capital and opened fresh political terrain upon which citizenship was to be negotiated with the post-colonial state. The condition of being 'refugee' was a significant tool to gain political influence and to bargain concessions from the new state – and therefore subject to negotiations that could enhance one's position in the new society. This is evident in the way a number of pressure groups and organizations were formed with the prefix refugee, such as 'Refugee Protection Society', 'All India Refugee Welfare Association' and 'Refugees Old Motor Parts Dealers Association' to name a few. It signified a moral community of victims and survivors of genocidal violence who were rendered homeless in the making of the post-colonial nation state. Second, while being 'refugee' formed the broad basis for negotiations with the state, it was the *social distinctions* – based on class, caste, gender, age and geography – within the displaced populations that shaped differing modes and outcomes of interaction with the governmental agencies in the different locations of the refugee camps and beyond. The word 'distinction' is used in a double sense to convey both *differences* and *privileges* accrued from differing levels of social capital accumulation that displaced individuals, families and communities possessed. At the bottom of this register of social distinctions were the state-dependent refugees who barely possessed any social capital or bargaining power to gain prime resources from the state agencies upon displacement. They were often the low caste groups, the rural and urban poor, and single women, who constituted the marginalized and who, consequently, had little influence on the ongoing political processes. At the top, on the other hand, were the *exceptions*, prominent men, and their families, often honoured and rewarded by the authorities for the services they rendered to the colonial state and whose experiences of movement did not always follow the standard narrative of loss and chaotic escape.[8] They depended on the state not for survival, but rather for recognition of their social eminence. They were resourceful, politically astute and well entrenched in useful social networks that came in handy while interacting with the state authorities. They were seen as natural leaders of the refugees and authentic representatives of 'refugee experiences' by the state authorities, even though sometimes their own experiences were far removed from those of the ordinary refugees they were representing. These individuals were drawn from *Rais* (pronounced *ra-ees*), or wealthy families, who traditionally took up specific social causes and performed community service and were often at the helm of political leadership; *sarkari afsar*, literally government officers, who were endowed with social prestige that came with their rank in the colonial administration; and middle-level prosperous traders, businessmen, teachers, local community leaders, who derived and magnified their authority from the community resettlement efforts they were engaged in.

In the following pages, I describe the everyday life of the refugees to show how: (a) the governmental imaginary of 'the refugee' became a powerful framing device for state policies that positioned the post-colonial state as an empathetic guardian of displaced people, as well as an all-too-visible screen behind which the state functionaries practised policy distinctively; (b) even as the displaced populations were defined through the state's imaginary of 'refugee', the label was actively appropriated, employed and given new meanings by the migrants themselves; and finally (c) the new citizenry was shaped distinctively in relation to refugees' degree of dependence on the state for survival and recognition.

IMAGINARY OF 'REFUGEE'

'Refugee' was the most popular term used in Indian newspapers, eyewitness accounts and statements by the political leadership to describe nearly ten million people who were forced to move into India by the internecine violence from mid-1947 onwards. It also formed a popular imaginary through which displaced people were now viewed as helpless, homeless and in need of rehabilitation. This view is fully reflected in Prime Minister Jawaharlal Nehru's description of these people as 'unfortunate refugees from Punjab and listening to their stories it is difficult not to be moved'.[9] An eyewitness account entitled 'Helpless Thousands in West Punjab' described 'thousands of Hindu and Sikh refugees ... depressed and half-starved, [all] but resigned'.[10] The newspapers were replete with heart-rending photos of men, women and children huddled in camps, cooking food at the roadside or just sleeping on pavements. A photo feature depicting the situation of refugees, entitled 'Influx of Refugees into Delhi', appeared with captions such as 'refugees arriving at the Delhi railway station', 'refugee receiving first aid treatment', 'two refugee families' and 'refugees receiving their rations'.[11] The very ordinary human activities of cooking, sleeping, sitting with one's family or just waiting in a queue had become special 'refugee' activities in this imaginary – each meant to underscore the plight and misfortune of the dislocated people.[12] The act of dislocation – matter out of place – had become the defining characteristic of the newcomers, and 'refugee' was the prism through which their everyday life was now described.[13] In other words, all previous identities and social distinctions were collapsed to constitute the 'refugee', an archetype of dislocated people in need of relocation within the post-colonial citizenry.

In the official Indian account entitled *The Story of Rehabilitation*, the 'refugee' is a generic product not of the state's failure to protect its citizens, but of 'a new and pernicious doctrine [that] had come to poison men's minds ... arson, rapine and murder were let loose [and] people were uprooted from their homes'.[14] The 'refugee' is a multitudinous body of 'five million people crazed with fear, shattered in body and mind, most of them pitifully destitute [who] had to be fed, clothed, protected from the ravages of disease, found shelter and homes, where they could be slowly nursed back to some semblance of lost dignity'.[15] Despite the occasional plural form used to describe the mass migration, the official narrative casts millions of individuals, a colossal demography, as a single multitude of being – anonymous, helpless, fearful and dispossessed subjects at the mercy of the state authorities for their bodily and moral healing.

The 'refugee' is also the raw material out of which modern citizens were produced, once the bodies had been healed and spirits restored in the refugee camps. We are told that 'when the refugee was sent back into the normal work-a-day world, *he* was restored and refreshed; discarding the crutches of the camp, *he* was able to respond to measures to make him indistinguishable from his fellow men, just another happy, useful citizen'.[16] The refugee body, for the purposes of policy-making, is a dispirited male body that can be repaired successfully, while the female bodies remain mostly absent, appearing only to signify the atrocities of sexual violence and abductions by the enemy. The refugee camps are the transformative spaces where governmental policies and practices of 'rehabilitation' bear fruit in recharging the broken spirits and incarnating a new citizenry.

The new label 'refugee' was also favoured by the displaced populations and often used interchangeably with Punjabi/Hindi terms like *panahgeer* and *sharnarthi*, literally meaning those in need of shelter and security. Despite the interchangeable usage in everyday parlance, 'refugee' was more than a literal expression of homelessness and insecurity and less than a full legal categorization in the administration of displaced people. The identity of refugee was affixed through official registration of displaced persons as refugees. This brief, though important, ritual was performed upon arrival, when a refugee card with name, registration number and date of arrival was issued. This card was essential proof in gaining a ration card, temporary and permanent housing, admission to educational institutions and employment earmarked for the Partition migrants. The state practice of formalizing identities through the issuing of a 'refugee card', as it was popularly known, became an important first step on the road to becoming a proper citizen-subject of the new state.

In legal terms, though, the word 'refugee' had little meaning since the actual laws pertaining to migrant property and compensation made use of terms like 'displaced person' or 'evacuee'.[17] The very usage of the term to describe displacement in official as well as academic discourse is instructive – especially when it was never employed in the legal sense. During India's Partition in 1947, the international legal mechanisms concerning refugees – or 'stateless' people – were still not in place, but the ideas and debates around refugees and nation states were commonplace.[18] The forced migrants to India (and Pakistan) were not stateless in the sense of in need of rights, since they were assured of citizenship rights upon arrival. The frequent usage seems to have had an emotive function, besides being a governmental technology of population classification, to draw attention to the helplessness and misery the migrants faced in everyday negotiations over resources such as food, housing, medical aid and employment opportunities. And, more importantly, it helped emphasize the state's generosity in helping the displaced populations to overcome their miserable situation.

TECHNOLOGY OF SELF-REHABILITATION

The core principle of the official resettlement policy was *self-rehabilitation*, that is, the ability to become a productive citizen of the new nation state without state intervention.[19] This governmental technology of making citizens out of refugees was based on two prerequisites: (a) being dislocated and (b) being able to survive without the state's help. While the act of dislocation was mired in violence, loss and defeat, the act of survival independent of the state indicated success in overcoming those defeats. This individual feat – of turning defeat into success – facilitated one's entry into the new citizenry and formed subjects worthy of the new nation. The emerging process was, however, fraught with contradictions and tensions: while those who owned sufficient social capital were in little need of prodding from the state to be self-reliant, those who had no capital had little choice but to depend on the state. In practice, this meant that those who did not need the state for basic subsistence on an everyday basis were better placed to make the transition to citizenship than those who depended on the state. Thus, the effectiveness of the policy of self-rehabilitation supported a constituency that was already resourceful in one way or another.

To begin with, the policy was based on the useful employment of able-bodied refugees, while women, the infirm and disabled people were left on the margins. The official stance was that 'every grown up and able bodied refugee had to be found gainful employment. No one willing to work could be denied an opportunity to earn a living.'[20] The minister for rehabilitation, Mohanlal Saksena (1948–50), expressed this vision while reflecting upon the problems of rehabilitation: 'the energy and courage, enterprise and self reliance of the displaced persons themselves led me to hope that it may be given to me to assist these stricken people, and uprooted millions, in their settlement; and if possible, in making them the pioneers of a new social order'.[21] The emphasis was on self-reliance and self-rehabilitation, though under the watchful eyes of the state authorities. Those who did not show the promise of self-reliance, that is, who needed financial support from the state, were chided for being 'lazy and feckless, losing all initiative, self-respect and self confidence'.[22] The 'free doles' were seen as a disincentive that had a demoralizing effect and were stopped soon after Mr Saksena took over the minister's office. He later wrote: 'paradoxical as it may seem, the discontinuance of gratuitous relief has been one of the biggest strokes of rehabilitation, for it gave the "drone" a shake up, and set him thinking as to how best to rehabilitate himself' (inverted commas in original).[23] The allusion to 'drone', a male honey bee, is significant with its double meanings of parasitic loafer living off others' labour as well as remote-controlled object that is not its own agent. The refugees who survived on cash handouts were necessarily seen as lazy and unmotivated, irrespective of other factors such as ill health or the inability to find employment, especially in a new location. The withdrawal of state support was seen as a necessary action that turned passive recipients of aid into active architects of their own destiny.

The ability to self-rehabilitate, it seems, was crucial in becoming an active citizen of the new nation. The success criterion of transcending refugee-ness was measured as: 'only when the displaced person has shed his dependence on government or private doles has he been fully rehabilitated'.[24] Often those able to look after themselves were the resourceful ones who had, for example, transferable government jobs that reinstated them upon movement, assets that could be liquidated or exchanged and capital to invest in new businesses. Those who could afford to support themselves seldom lived in refugee camps for long periods. In fact, the government had created two types of refugee housing facilities – self-supported and state supported. The newcomers arriving at the refugee registration office in Delhi, for example, were asked if they could afford their own food and clothing rations.[25] If they could, then they were assigned the concrete-built old military barracks, while others were sent to camps where cloth tents from the Second World War were used. From the very moment of arrival, an administrative filter was created that weeded out resource-rich people from the mass of refugees. Thus, those left within the camps were the socially weakest groups in comparison to those who could earn their livelihood independently of state aid. Mr Saksena, in fact, gave credit to the 'displaced persons, especially outside camps, that … have made a supreme effort to earn their livelihood and to stand on their own feet. Many of them have done remarkably well in rehabilitating themselves without the aid of the Government.'[26] The physical distance from the state-run refugee camps was clearly seen as a sign of forward movement towards being a full citizen.

This approach, however, left out women and disabled and infirm people without family support networks from the possibility of fully forsaking state support and, consequently, becoming self-rehabilitated full citizens of India. At the end of his report on refugee rehabilitation, Mr Saksena wrote a chapter called 'miscellaneous problems – unattached women etc.' where the fate of single women is discussed sympathetically. While he earlier insisted that refugees be put to work to achieve rehabilitation, here he pre-empted any discussion by circumscribing the women as a 'permanent liability' to the state.[27] He explained that 'from the very beginning the Government of India have [sic] undertaken responsibility for the maintenance and care of women and children' and that this should continue to be 'a responsibility of the state'.[28] Unattached women were wards of the state, to be protected and cared for in the absence of family or a male guardian. The state took its role as a patriarch seriously enough to construct exclusive camps for unattached women that kept the inmates in seclusion. For example, Kasturba Niketan camp in the Lajpat Nagar area of Delhi was secured with high barbed wire and guarded round the clock so that no male intruders could enter the premises.[29] The camp protocol did not even allow male visitors inside the private lodgings. This seclusion of unattached women, often young widows, was in keeping with the contemporary norms of controlling female sexuality and avoiding socially unsanctioned reproduction.[30] The young unattached women were considered unsafe outside the protective control of family or state. There were not many avenues for these women to self-rehabilitate and shed their dependence upon the state. The resettlement policies were largely tailored to meet the needs of an ideal type, i.e. the able-bodied, masculine refugee. The frequent use of the masculine pronoun in official writings suggests that the object of the state's gaze was primarily the male refugee – the female refugees were deemed to be included within that archetype. The 'unattached' women, kept in seclusion and guarded by a patriarchal state, had few options to become independent of the state.

STATE OF DEPENDENCE

The paradoxes within the self-rehabilitation policy are best viewed on the premises of the now defunct Ministry of Relief and Rehabilitation.[31] The ministry ceased to exist in 1965, when officially the rehabilitation work was considered finished even though the settlement of claims was far from over. The unfinished work was entrusted to a new department of rehabilitation, formed with the objective of completing the 'residual work of rehabilitation'. This administrative move suggested that resettlement, at least in the eyes of the state, had been concluded and that whatever was left unfinished was a mere residue unworthy of full attention. Yet, during my fieldwork, the queues at the premises of the rehabilitation department suggested that not only had the resettlement programmes never been fully concluded, but also the old men and women waiting in the queues had never been able to fulfil the official goal of self-rehabilitation. More than five decades later, they were still making regular trips to the resettlement office to get their 'cases' settled. This ageing generation now constituted the *residue* of the Partition upheaval – made to wait for long hours and dealt with impatiently by young officers who had little comprehension of events which, from their point of view, belonged to history.

I met Kewal Ram and his wife, Kanta Devi, at the resettlement office during my routine visits to consult the department's record room. Both were in their late sixties and had moved, together with their respective families, from Lahore to Delhi in 1947 at the height of the violence. They started their lives anew in a refugee camp located at the historic site of Kingsway that had been built in connection with the 1911 Delhi Durbar in honour of King George V. The camp was a basic facility where the inhabitants were given bare minimum rations and financial aid for a limited period. This particular camp housed those who had no private means of support and necessarily had to depend on the state. Both their families, Kewal Ram's and his wife's, had lost whatever they had owned, since they were forced to leave Lahore in haste. Kewal Ram's father used to run a store selling everyday household items in the locality where they lived. The shop was a rented property and that meant they had no claim to commercial property in lieu of property lost in Lahore. Their only hope was to have a rentable shop allotted to them by the government since it was impossible to buy property in Delhi because of the sky-high property prices. The situation was made worse because better-off migrants had already begun purchasing commercial and residential property in Delhi, reportedly at exorbitant prices. A news report suggested that premises in Delhi were being 'acquired by Lahore businessmen by paying *pagris* ("premium") ranging between Rupees 50,000–100,000'.[32] These were enormous sums for ordinary people, who could not compete in an open market to acquire assets in order to earn their livelihood. Kewal Ram's father was told that he could rent a shop if any were left after the disbursement of property claims had been dealt with. In the meantime, the father and son began hawking homemade *pakoras* (lentil snacks) in the neighbourhood colonies to make ends meet. They would regularly return, without fail, to the resettlement office to enquire about the possibility of renting a shop. The years passed, and Kewal Ram's father died without ever re-creating his Lahore shop in Delhi; the responsibility for running the family fell upon his son. After persistent pleas, in the early 1960s the family, now consisting of the young couple's four daughters and mother, was allotted a two-room flat in the newly constructed Old Double storey area of Lajpat Nagar. They had started their hawking business again, even though it was tougher now since they lived far away from the city in a sparsely inhabited area.

When I met the couple in 2002, they were waiting outside the office for their turn to argue their case for the shop that had been promised to Kewal Ram's father in the late 1940s. Since I was working on the 'history' of Partition, I was not expecting to meet people who were still arguing their decades-old cases before the settlement officer. Yet each person in the queue had a different story to tell – about withheld pensions, promised accommodation or jobs, unsettled compensation claims, among other things – that indicated that their lives were not settled even though decades had lapsed. Partition was not history for them; they were living its consequences in their everyday lives. In fact, the archive at the resettlement office is called a 'record room' and not an archive, I was told, because 'cases were still live' and so cannot be officially designated an archive.[33] Kewal Ram showed me his refugee registration card that he had carefully kept all these years, along with a bundle of official letters concerning his plea. The refugee card was the sole evidence he had to testify to his claims of dislocation and all the hardships that followed it.

I asked them why they continued to pursue their case after all these years, especially when there was little indication that the plea would be entertained. The answer was simple – it was a matter of earning a livelihood, as they had no pension or family support that would take care of them. Their daughters had been married off and were unable to look after them because of pressure from their husbands' families. Their only income was what they earned from the makeshift stall they had set up some years before. On compassionate grounds, and with due intervention from the local municipal councillor, the couple had been allowed to put up a stall near the newly established Central Market in Lajpat Nagar by the municipal authorities. This arrangement was ended in the early 2000s when the municipality decided to demolish all 'unauthorized' structures in the area in an effort to curb illegal constructions.[34]

Their stall was found to be an unauthorized structure by the municipality and was removed. This fresh setback was the reason why they went back to the settlement office to find out if they could pursue their livelihood legally in a rented shop. The answer was a clear 'no', as they soon found out, because the settlement office did not have any jurisdiction over the municipality. It no longer had the mandate or resources to make such decisions, especially after the department had been amalgamated within a larger full-fledged ministry.

The clerk at the settlement office, whom I interacted with everyday, told me that these people wasted everyone's time by pressing on with useless cases.[35] He would helpfully draw my attention to the well-known 'success stories' of refugees who, through sheer hard work, had built their fortunes.[36] In contrast, the people who queued up at his office had somehow failed to show the same initiative that made success out of failure. They were still looking to the state for support after many decades, long after most other refugees had taken control of their lives. The lack of enthusiasm among the officials was compounded by the fact that the department was to be downsized further. Most were waiting to be transferred to other departments that were considered active and relevant. The resettlement department had ceased to be relevant in the larger scheme of things, even though it remained relevant to people like Kewal Ram whose most important possession was a refugee card. The only capital he owned was the moral capital of being a refugee, which he strategically employed in an effort to gain a foothold in his old age.

While Kewal Ram and his family had moved out of the refugee camp, they hardly possessed any tools to be self-reliant outside the camp. Though at a policy level refugees were to be given loans to start businesses, in practice it was difficult to obtain them since one needed guarantees and references from community leaders to safeguard the loan. It was especially difficult for people like Kewal Ram who clearly did not have important social connections or any property in lieu of which they could make a claim to assets like better off refugees. The most they had been able to manage was a makeshift stall near the market through the interventions of their local councillor. This too was taken away from them since the stall had never been legally endorsed. They had not shown qualities of self-reliance that would make them citizens befitting the new nation. At the same time, their own efforts at becoming meaningful citizens – by attempting to start small business – were frequently thwarted by various governmental authorities. Their stories did not fit in the popular 'failure-to-success' narrative, and neither did they make the crucial 'refugee-to-citizen' transition by distancing themselves from state dependence.

THE RELIABLE SELF

Though the contemporary discourse on refugees, at the time of Partition, was mostly sympathetic in drawing popular attention to the 'plight' of the generic refugee, very few discursive fragmentations were made to highlight social differences within the migrant population. This is why the following news report, entitled 'The Ways of Rich Refugees', stands out as exceptional in its description of upper-class refugees:

they buy the best of everything without regard for the prices. From 2 p.m., provided the weather is not too bad, they begin to go up and down the Mall, the men talking about their losses in Lahore and the women about the dresses and fancy goods they had to leave behind. There are a number of restaurants on the Mall which every evening are filled with bored, well-dressed men and women. You cannot mistake the look on these refugee faces. While some are thus killing time, others roam the Mall looking for officials of the East Punjab Government, members of the Legislative Assembly, retired judges and others. From them they get the latest information from Lahore. This information is then embellished and passed on from one group to another. Highly coloured accounts of disturbances causing dismay and demoralization are thus passed on as factual news. In this mood of self-pity the refugees look for people to blame and find their own leaders the handiest.[37]

The above is one of the very few newspaper reports that focused on the wealthier sections of the migrant population. These refugees, compared to the camp refugees, were able not only to meet their everyday needs of food and shelter on their own, but could even afford to maintain their normal lifestyle in exile. They regret their losses and speculate about the 'disturbances' taking place in the plains – of which they have little direct knowledge. They appear more as spectators than actors in the Partition drama. This theme of loss had become a meme through which one could recount, embellish and impress others of the riches one owned. Even this moment of suffering could be turned into a technique of reification of one's social status. The theme of loss and the detailed recounting of all the wealth that had been left behind were frequent themes I encountered among the upper-class refugees in Delhi during my fieldwork. In contrast, the lower middle-class refugees were often less detailed about their losses and would rather gloss over the subject completely. This contrast made sense, after my initial surprise, since one had to own something in the first place in order to lose it. The lower middle class and the poorer sections of, for example, untouchables had few assets and consequently a more limited discourse of loss. Clearly, the upper classes were not the target section of the state's policy of self-rehabilitation since the wealthy migrants had sufficient means to live without state intervention. Many of them had escaped violence in cities like Lahore and Delhi by moving to hill resorts long before the riots broke out at the onset of summer.[38] This also happened to be the season when the elite – high-ranking government officials, merchants and big landowners among others – traditionally migrated to the cooler climate of the hills along with the annual migration of the colonial government.[39] The migrant population in this news report, unlike the inhabitants of the refugee camps, was well versed in the ways the state machinery functioned, which put them in an advantageous position to begin with. Similarly, their personal acquaintance with the state officials and policy-makers was an asset that could be employed when resettling businesses and families in the new place.

A good example of social networking to gain resources is underscored in the following letter to Minister of Rehabilitation M.L. Saksena from one Mrs Kamla Kaushal asking for an allotment of a bungalow plot in the posh environs of the newly developed Nizamuddin colony in lieu of lost property in Pakistan. These plots were much in demand and were, in fact, a source of conflict between the Old Fort camp refugees and the authorities since the former were initially promised allotments in the colony.[40] The letter begins in rather deferential, though direct, terms:

> I beg to apply for one of the larger plots in Nizamuddin area. I am [a] refugee from NWFP and a widow having lost my husband during the communal riots in 1947 at Bannu. I beg to state that I was allotted one of the Pusa Road hutments, which I surrendered requesting at the same time that I should be given a plot of land. Last of all I beg to state that I have been labouring and tilling in the Nizamuddin area and I hope that work shall not be ignored. In this connection it may be added that I was photographed with Mrs Saksena [the Minister's wife] and other ladies while working in that area and the photo appeared in the Illustrated Weekly [a magazine] of that month.[41]

Mrs Kaushal signed off this letter from an address located in the upmarket locality of Connaught Place rather than a refugee camp. The most important identity, however, to gain the plot was that of a refugee, since the locality was being developed for the resourceful refugees. An official note invited 'displaced persons from Western Pakistan who are gainfully employed in Delhi' to submit bids for the 60 x 116 ft plots.[42] The bid could be placed against compensation certificates issued by the Ministry in lieu of property lost in Pakistan. Those refugees who were neither gainfully employed nor in possession of compensation certificates were not eligible for the plot allotments. The fact that Mrs Kaushal became a widow during the Partition violence formed the emotive context of her plea. She states in her letter that she gave up the Pusa Road 'hutments', which were quarter of the size of the bungalows, in the hope of a larger bungalow plot. She mentions that she had been 'labouring and tilling' [sic] the land,[43] and, most importantly, that she had been photographed with the Minister's wife, who had visited the area. This last bit of information makes the plea more interesting since the photograph with Mrs Saksena constitutes the most emphatic argument forwarded in order to secure the plot. This last argument took up at least as much space as her being a refugee and a widow in her case for the plot. Clearly, Mrs Kaushal believed that this important bit of additional information would strengthen her chances of securing a plot. Whether the strategy worked or not is unclear since further correspondence on her plea is missing from the files. But what is clear is that social connections were seen as an important tool in gaining a foothold in the new place.

The needs and strategies of the elite refugees were, clearly, different from those of the ordinary refugees. The common thread was the emotive frame of being 'refugee', despite differing experiences, which prefaced all demands for houses, promotions and easy loans. An exchange of correspondence between Devi Dayal, a high-ranking bureaucrat from the Ministry of External Affairs, and the Ministry of Rehabilitation highlights this contrast. Devi Dayal was allotted one of the much-coveted plots in the Nizamuddin area in 1949. Far from being happy, he wrote a long letter to the Ministry of Rehabilitation complaining about his situation and asking for an easy loan to construct his house on the plot. In the letter he begins by emphasizing his status as a registered refugee, even though a little later he explains his migration as a 'regular transfer' that brought him to India. It was a common practice of the state to arrange job transfers from Pakistan to India (and vice versa) for its employees. A special Transfer Bureau was set up for this purpose as early as 1947.[44] This way, the employees did not lose their monthly income, accommodation, provident funds or any pensions upon migration. His complaints included the following:

> By transfer to India, I have lost 22 years [of] permanent service; I have till now not been paid the balance in my Provident Fund; I lost all my movable and immovable property in Pakistan and have not received any compensation or rehabilitation facilities; I have four children receiving expensive education in schools and colleges but have not obtained any loan, advance, scholarship or other concession from public funds in aid of their education.[45]

The list of grievances was a bit exaggerated and contradictory since, under the transfer rules, employees did not lose seniority and were looked upon rather sympathetically by the state. The provident funds were paid to all employees upon transfer, as agreed under the terms of transfer. Paradoxically, Devi Dayal claims not to have received any compensation against lost property, even though his letter was occasioned by the allotment of a bungalow plot for the same. His letter also states that his children continued to receive an expensive education, though he complains about not having received any aid to subsidize it. This last bit is specially striking since for the vast majority basic survival – food and shelter – was at stake, rather than seeking subsidies to finance expensive private education. For most ordinary refugees, a regular income, accommodation and the undisrupted education of their children were more of a luxury than a requirement. In Devi Dayal's account, one does not witness the events of violence and chaos that constitute many Partition accounts. Partition was the occasion of his movement to India, not a constant determinant in his life as a post-colonial citizen. This letter basically showed how very different spheres of reality existed in the otherwise generalized universe of refugees.

Although refugees like Devi Dayal had little experience of the hardships implied by the label 'refugee', the 'plight of refugees' was a frequent meme used by the elite to mobilize refugees into a political force. In 1949 the Refugee Protection Society (RPS) decided to field 'refugee' candidates in the state Assembly elections since the government was not seen as doing enough to rehabilitate refugees. Charges of negligence had long been levelled against the government by refugees dependent upon the state for loans and the allotment of housing etc. In a letter addressed to RPS President Diwan Chaman Lall, a wealthy barrister from the Punjab and a refugee, a society member noted the problem as follows:

> dissatisfaction has very much increased amongst the refugees and they openly charge that the Government has failed to solve the problem even to a negligible degree. Some of the more enthusiastic among them even doubt the intentions of the Government. This, however, seems to be more due to a *sense of desperation* rather than a true picture of the facts.[46]

While describing the sense of neglect and desperation felt by refugees in need of state support, the writer refers to the refugees as 'them', thereby clearly separating himself (and the RPS) from the ordinary refugees. The lamentations of the refugees are seen as exaggerations not based on true facts. Even while representing the refugees' state, the writer seems to be an arbiter between the refugees and the government rather than a partisan voice of the refugees.

The list of twenty-three election candidates suggested by the society underscores this distance between the refugees and their representatives. To begin with, a number of them are variously described as 'refugee business magnate', 'important refugee industrialist', 'refugee merchant', 'refugee businessman' and 'refugee leader', among others.[47] Such descriptions carry inbuilt paradoxes that, at once, convey social prestige, economic power and influence conjoined with the emotive and helpless state of being 'refugee'. Interestingly, none of the candidates actually lived in the refugee camps; instead, a number of their addresses were located in the fashionable district of Connaught Place. Their financial losses were minimal since there were private agencies that sold or exchanged evacuee property in both India and Pakistan.[48] In any case, the state policy of compensation made it possible to make good one's losses provided one had the proper documentation and a bit of patience. Most of the candidates were high profile individuals, well-established businessmen, political leaders, wealthy philanthropists, influential community leaders and professional doctors and lawyers. The only common bond they had with the refugees whose experiences they were representing was formed by the act of dislocation and the official refugee identity cards they had been issued with. This mobilization did not lead to a political formation but became a fertile ground from where 'distinguished' members of the refugee community emerged to provide leadership and direction.[49] They were successful examples of the state's policy of becoming good citizens – as they had been self-reliant and productive from an early stage. But they also represented the hollowness of the state's vision since their supposed transformative journeys – of turning failure into success and thus gaining a meaningful place in the new citizenry – had not always been travelled. Their abridged journeys, if anything, created unfavourable contrasts with those who had to struggle for basic survival in their everyday lives.

PERFORMING CITIZENSHIP

The refugee registration card, in the historical trajectory of self-rehabilitation, carries a particular significance. While it generally symbolized the official recognition of one's dislocation and earned concessions and resources from the state, it also conveyed a state of helplessness and dependence for some whose journeys had been turbulent and difficult. To others still, such as Devi Dayal and Diwan Chaman Lall, the acquisition of refugee cards was a legible entry into borrowed 'refugee experiences' and concessions even when their own journeys did not bear much resemblance to the popular narratives of forced movement. These differing meanings invested in refugee cards were made apparent when a former resident of Rawalpindi narrated his personal story of movement, homelessness and long struggles to me. At the end of his narration, which took place in front of his two sons, he offered to show me his refugee card, which he had kept but never shown to anyone. The card was meaningless in his current life, except for its historical value. As I waited for him to return, I overheard his younger son arguing fervently against his offer to show me the card. A little later, the son returned to say that his father could not find his refugee card. When the father returned, he shrugged off his futile search by suggesting it did not matter since they were not refugees anymore.

The card, clearly, was an uncomfortable reminder of a difficult and often inglorious past, and a matter of disagreement within the family. Whether the card went missing or was hidden wilfully, its absence signified its irrelevance for the family more than five decades later. The family over the years had gained success in business and could choose to keep or dispense with this relic from the past. They had been able to self-rehabilitate themselves, and therefore their refugee identity was no longer central to them. However, this option was not available to Kewal Ram, for whom the card was a necessary proof of identity when he interacted with the state authorities. In the eyes of the state, he had failed to be a success since he continued knocking on the doors of different authorities even after five decades.

The core principle of the state's refugee rehabilitation policies was self-rehabilitation – aided and initiated by the state but to be self-executed by the refugees in order to become well-integrated citizens of India. The idea of self-rehabilitation, in fact, carried within it two seemingly complementary processes – of *being made* independent of the state, though upon the state's insistence, and *becoming* self-reliant through one's active efforts. Both processes worked simultaneously towards a common goal of relocating the newcomers on the citizenship map, yet they carried tensions and different outcomes from the very beginning. While some refugees – owners of social and economic capitals – were able to *become* self-reliant from the start, others who did not have resources had to *be made* independent by the state. Kewal Ram belonged to the latter category of refugees who did not grow out of the shadows of the state. While the officials at the resettlement office found his pleas a waste of time and categorized him a failure, it was hardly a matter of debate that the state had failed him not only by not focusing on his needs, but also by thwarting his attempts to begin small-scale independent ventures.

The state's attention, from the very beginning, had been on resourceful refugees. These individuals and groups were not beholden to the state for their everyday existence since they owned private means and social networks of support. Even though their journeys had little in common with the stories of violence, mayhem and shortages of food and water along the way, they were not only seen as representatives of the refugee experience but also considered leaders of refugee communities. Thus, being labelled 'refugee', and a self-reliant one at that, was to be given a desirable identity that helped integrate the newcomers in the upper echelons of the host society. This way one could draw upon the moral capital invested in the imaginary of refugee – without having experienced the hardships and struggles popularly associated with it – and yet be seen as an ideal example of a self-reliant refugee based on one's own social capital.

Three conclusions may be drawn to sum up the discussions above. First, while there was universal sympathy for an archetype of refugee – hardworking but fallen on bad times – this did not always translate into concrete support since individuals seldom match the ideal. The mythical persona of refugee was actually constitutive of a wide range of distinctions, whereas the state policies were made following the one-size-fits-all principle. Second, one's position as a post-colonial citizen was shaped by the relationship one had with the state: the greater one's ability to be self-reliant, the better one's chances of gaining a firm foothold in the new citizenry. Finally, it was not only the state-dependents who were enchanted with state power; it was also the self-reliant refugees who appealed to the state for recognition of their social eminence and advancement. Self-rehabilitation was not always a display of initiative and hard work, but often an expression of resourcefulness in manoeuvring the authorities in everyday life. The policy of self-rehabilitation, in fact, inadvertently rewarded those who owned social capital and could manage on their own, rather than supporting those who really needed state help. Those left on the margins of the new citizenry symbolized the state's failure to design policies that focused on the most needy and subaltern of the refugees.

NOTES

1. Joya Chatterji, 'Rights or Charity? Government and Refugees: The Debate of Relief and Rehabilitation 1947–50', in Suvir Kaul (ed.), *Partition of Memory: The Afterlife of the Division of India* (Delhi, 2001).
2. See Ravinder Kaur, 'Narrative Absence: The Untouchable Account of Partition Migration', *Contributions to Indian Sociology*, 42(2) (2008), pp. 281–306, and also *Since 1947: Partition Narratives among Punjabi Migrants of Delhi* (Delhi, 2007).
3. I draw upon Bourdieu's work on social capital here. See Pierre Bourdieu, *Distinctions: A Social Critique of the Judgement of Taste* (Cambridge, MA, 1984).
4. The fieldwork in Delhi was conducted over different periods in 2001–2, 2005 and 2007.
5. The citizenship rights of the displaced people from Pakistan were guaranteed in retrospect under Part II (clauses 5 and 6) of the Constitution of India adopted on 26 January 1950. According to the rules, all those who had 'migrated to the territory of India from the territory now included in Pakistan shall be deemed citizens of India at the commencement of this constitution'. The cut-off date for this provision was 19 July 1948, after which special registration had to be undertaken. This did not mean that migration took place in one clean sweep since people often travelled back and forth, unable to decide where to settle down. This is borne out by numerous records of litigation over property with the office of the Custodian General of Evacuee Property. See Syed Mohammad Husain, *The Law and Practice Relating to Evacuee Property in India* (Delhi, 1954).
6. Thomas H. Marshall, *Citizenship and Social Class and Other Essays* (Cambridge, 1950).
7. Aihwa Ong, *Buddha Is Hiding: Refugees, Citizenship, the New America* (Berkeley, CA, 2003), p. 276.
8. On state patronage and the making of the new elite during the colonial period, see Francis Robinson, 'Consultation and Control: The United Provinces' Government and Its Allies, 1860–1906', *Modern Asian Studies*, 5(4) (1971), pp. 313–36.
9. *Hindustan Times*, 29 August 1947.
10. *Hindustan Times*, 2 September 1947.
11. Ibid.
12. See Liisa Malkki on representations of refugees in *Purity and Exile: Violence, Memory and Exile in National Cosmology of Hutu Refugees in Tanzania* (Chicago, 1992).
13. See Mary Douglas Douglas, *Purity and Danger: An Analysis of the Concepts of Pollution and Danger* (London, 2002).

14. U.A. Rao, *The Story of Rehabilitation*, Ministry of Information and Broadcasting, Government of India (Delhi, 1967), p. 3.

15. Ibid., p. 36.

16. Ibid., p. 47.

17. See, for example, *East Punjab Evacuee (Administration Property) Ordinance of 1947* (Delhi, 14 September 1947), where the legal terminology of 'displaced persons' and 'evacuees' is first proposed and explained. In contrast, the official accounts of Partition migration and resettlement are constructed around 'refugees'. See, for example, reports such as *Millions on the Move: The Aftermath of Partition* (Delhi, undated) and U.B. Rao, *The Story of Rehabilitation*, both issued by the Ministry of Information and Broadcasting, Government of India.

18. The sixteenth-century expression 'refugee', used for French Huguenot groups in exile, denotes individuals and groups seeking refuge to escape threats and persecution in their homeland. The term was imbued with specific legal meanings and status when the United Nations High Commission for Refugees (UNHCR) was established in 1950, followed by the ratification of the Refugee Convention a year later. See *Convention and Protocol Relating to the Status of Refugees* (Geneva, 1951 and 1976), http://www.unhcr.org/protect/PROTECTION/3b66c2aa10.pdf (accessed 4 May 2009).

19. The idea of self-rehabilitation is expressed in official documents in terms of self-reliance, or the ability or intent to rehabilitate oneself. See, for example, Mohan Lal Saksena, *Some Reflections on the Problems of Rehabilitation* (Delhi, undated). Also Rao, *The Story of Rehabilitation*.

20. Rao, p. 63.

21. Saksena, p.2.

22. Saksena, p. 3.

23. Saksena, pp. 3–4.

24. Rao, p. 62.

25. Interview with V.K. Kataria, Delhi, 16 December 2000.

26. Saksena, p. 33.

27. Saksena, p. 125

28. Saksena, pp. 125–7.

29. Interview with Rajrani, Delhi, 10 February 2002.

30. Kaur, *Since 1947*, p. 147.

31. The Ministry of Relief and Rehabilitation was set up in September 1947, and in 1965 it was integrated within the Ministry of Home Affairs as the Department of Relief and Rehabilitation. See Rao, *The Story of Rehabilitation*.

32. *Hindustan Times*, 21 August 1947.

33. 'Archive', here, seems to bear a sense of something that is no longer relevant in everyday life and can, therefore, be consigned to professional history writers. Interview with Sham Singh, Record Room attendant at the Department of Rehabilitation, Delhi, February 2002.

34. The demolition drive in Delhi was the result of a Supreme Court directive to the Municipal Corporation of Delhi to remove illegal constructions and extensions.

35. My repeated visits meant that at least the functionaries in the lower echelons of the departments had become friendly enough to explain and provide a context, as they saw it, to the predictable drama everyday.

36. This was a popular theme at the department, where a few individual success stories were repeatedly narrated to underscore the different destinies shaped by hard work or the lack of it. The favourite rags-to-riches story was that of the hotelier H.S. Oberoi, the late owner of Oberoi hotel chain, who had come to Delhi penniless and then become an international

success. In fact, the flagship hotel of this chain was a stone's throw from the settlement office, and that perhaps explained the excessive emphasis on Oberoi's story. However, success stories like that of Oberoi were far and few between and not a general trend.

37. *Hindustan Times*, 31 August 1947.

38. The Partition violence took place in different time periods and different locations. The first major series of violent acts was reported from Rawalpindi in March 1947, followed by widespread violence in Lahore in May and then Delhi in August and September. The Rawalpindi violence had, in fact, initiated pre-emptive migration by minority groups, namely Hindus and Sikhs, seeking security in areas considered safe. For the chronology and nature of Partition violence, see Anders Bjørn Hansen, *Partition and Genocide: Manifestations of Violence in Punjab 1937–47* (Delhi, 2002).

39. The colonial government in Delhi moved to Shimla every summer since the heat was found too oppressive to conduct administrative business.

40. I explore in detail the conflict over plot allotments in Nizamuddin in Kaur, *Since 1947*, ch. 4.

41. Letter from Mrs Kamla Kaushal to the Minister of Relief and Rehabilitation, file no. RHB/120(3)/49, dated 2 November 1949, National Archives, Delhi.

42. 'Bungalow Plots for Sale to Displaced Persons in Nizamuddin Colony', press note from the Ministry of Rehabilitation, file no. RHB/120(3)/49, undated.

43. The Old Fort camp refugees had been initially asked to provide manual labour to prepare the land for construction. Many believed that they would be given the land they were working on. This explains Mrs Kaushal's emphasis on tilling the land.

44. Annual Report 1947–8, Ministry of Relief and Rehabilitation, Government of India.

45. Letter from Devi Dayal to Mehr Chand Khanna, adviser to the Minister of Relief and Rehabilitation, file no. RHB/120(3)/49, dated 28 November 1949.

46. Diwan Chaman Lall Papers, file no. 73/1949, dated 28 July 1948.

47. Diwan Chaman Lall Papers, file no. 73/1949, undated.

48. Letter from Durga Das & Co. detailing commission rates and terms of business, Diwan Chaman Lall Papers, file no. 73/1949.

49. For example, Mehar Chanda Khanna, a refugee and political leader from North-West Frontier Province, was appointed as Minister of Relief and Rehabilitaion in 1950 as a result of pressure from refugee interest groups.

'HOW MANY MORE FRAGMENTS?' (*AUR KITNE TUKDE*)

EXPLORING GENDERED VIOLENCE ON PARTITION(ED) WOMEN IN THEATRE

Lata Singh

Indian Institute of Advanced Study, Shimla

ABSTRACT　This article critically engages with a contemporary play, *Aur Kitne Tukde*, staged in the Hindi language in various cities and towns in India and Pakistan, about gendered violence during Partition. It unsettles the master narrative of 'honour', 'martyrdom', 'choice' and women's 'agency' on Partition. The article also highlights the significance of the play in breaking the silences around Partition in the theatre, which, as compared with other cultural and literary mediums, reaches out to a larger section of people in unique ways. It underlines how the whole production of the play was a process of traversing and sharing the journey and trauma of Partition not only for the actors but also for the audiences. The article also tries to problematize the whole question of violence and its representation.

Keywords: Partition, theatre, honour, choice, violence, martyrdom

The departure of the British from India was accompanied by a bloody Partition in which one million people perished and over ten million were displaced in the largest peacetime mass migration recorded in the twentieth century. Widespread killings, looting, abductions and rape became inseparable features of this forced migration of Hindus, Muslims and Sikhs in the west and Hindus and Muslims in the east. For a long time, however, Partition historiography continued to concentrate on the events, causations, negotiations and state policies, overlooking the human dimensions. In fact, the abundance of political histories on Partition was paralleled by the paucity of social histories of this painful ordeal. This is a curious and somewhat inexplicable circumstance, that an event of such tremendous societal impact and importance had been passed over virtually in silence by the social sciences. However, in the last decade or so scholars and activists have revisited this traumatic history and sought to excavate its lived experience, largely through recovering the testimonies of the survivors.[1]

Women's voices, in times of conflict such as the 1947 tragedy, had also remained submerged despite the fact that around 75,000 women were estimated to have been abducted and raped by men of various religious communities. Women often figure as objects of study rather than as subjects – present yet invisible; their experience of this

Address for correspondence: Lata Singh, D-13, Retreat Appts, Patparganj, I.P. Extn., Delhi – 110092, India. E-mail: lata_singh@hotmail.com

Cultural and Social History, Volume 6, Issue 4, pp. 447–466 © The Social History Society 2009
DOI 10.2752/147800409X466281

historic event has been neither properly examined nor assigned any historical value. This is not to valorize experience over other equally important considerations, but rather to recognize that it adds a critical dimension to any analysis. It helps us to understand the impact of such an event on men and women, on relations between them, and between gender and social and historical processes. Recent works that have rewritten Partition history from a gender perspective have been providing, for the first time, testimonies and memories of women caught in the turmoil of the events. Women are made not only visible but central, by looking at the general experience of violence, dislocation and displacement from a gendered perspective. The women's accounts are vivid with memories of loss and violence, the experience of abduction and widowhood, of rehabilitation and, sometimes, even liberation. These works explore what country, nation and religious identity mean for women, and they address the question of the nation state and the gendering of citizenship.[2]

This article is based on a contemporary Indian play called *Aur Kitne Tukde*, written and staged in the Hindi language, which translates as 'How Many More Fragments?'. The play explores issues surrounding the gendered violence during Partition.[3] The source of the play was Urvashi Butalia's book *The Other Side of Silence*, a collection of stories, interviews and recollections of the people who survived Partition. The play revolves around the stories of four women – otherwise unconnected but brought together by the commonality of their experiences during and after Partition. It was first staged in Delhi in 2001 and taken to many parts of the country and also to Pakistan. It provides an example of the holocausts that have continued to haunt the world of art and literature. In the Western world there has been a substantial body of literature, art, films and plays on the Holocaust, highlighting its sufferings and horrors. However, in India by contrast, except in the creative medium of literature, the cultural media have not responded in a significant way to Partition. Literature has recorded the full horror of Partition, the greater part of which was written in the period immediately following the division of the country. Popular sentiment and perception, as reflected in Partition literature almost without exception, registered the fact of Partition with despair or anger and profound unhappiness.[4] But one is troubled, as is the director of this play, as to why the cultural media in India did not respond to or try to understand the crisis of the Partition holocaust as compared to the Holocaust in the Western world. The director, before taking up the play, wondered whether this silence had something to do with the medium of art itself or popular mentalities. The silence is better understood in the larger context of Partition. Many fleeing migrants wanted to suppress their memories of Partition because of the nature of gendered violence.[5] Often they had a lot to hide, and a lot to lose by publicly recounting what had happened to them. For instance, tens of thousands of women were abducted at the time and forcibly married into the households of men belonging to another faith. Some abducted women were later 'returned' against their will, through an agreement between the Indian and Pakistani governments. Many had converted to another religion and hence wished to conceal their former identities. The prospect of digging up a troubled past is not one that people welcome willingly. There is also the question of how to approach the people who themselves committed acts of violence. Unlike in the Holocaust, where the aggressors and the victims were clearly identifiable, in the course of Partition very often people who were victims themselves committed acts of unthinkable violence against members of their own families. Violence was perpetrated by ordinary people on other ordinary people. Many men had murdered their own mothers, wives and sisters to protect the 'honour' of the community.[6] Another reason for the silence in the world of theatre could be the conventions of performance and representation, which have been blatantly patriarchal for a long time. Women's relationship with theatre has been problematic and tenuous.

INDIAN WOMEN AND THEATRE: BREAKING THE MOULD

In this context, the production by Kirti Jain is a significant attempt in the theatre to fill in the silences surrounding the gendered violence during Partition. Theatre is a very important cultural medium because of its potentiality for establishing direct and verbal lines of communication with a large audience. Live interaction with the viewers generates an immediate response, bringing to life social realities. Hence theatre could become an invigorating arena for cultural resistance – a potentially subversive cultural medium of expression – and consequently an important political site. It is a known fact that whenever there has been extreme repression imposed on people, theatre has provided a space to give voice to protest.[7] In India the medium of theatre as a tool for communication is very effective owing to the low levels of literacy in the country. In a largely non-literate culture, printed material reaches only the small percentage of the educated elite and guides the moral universe of only a minority, that is, the elite. Subaltern voices remain invisible in printed, written and official narratives. Oral cultural forms, which constitute an important part of the cultural life of the people, are integral to the retrieval of subaltern voices. Dramatic performances may not hold up to the exacting, critical categories of the social sciences due to their non-verbal nature, but these very novel languages, which are gestural, kinetic, expressive, farcical and ritualistic, offer a very different site for the emergence of subaltern voices.

Theatre has been impacted by radical Left-oriented Indian movements, which, with a veritable explosion of creativity and counter-culture, energized the medium by affecting a far-reaching change in both its concept and practice. Among other things, theatre became bolder, more innovative, more flexible, more portable, more community based and, above all, more concerned with the material and emotional life of its audience. The women's movement, one of the important streams of the radical movements, has significantly influenced women's theatre. In women's theatre a great awareness of the several levels at which a woman lives her life is becoming visible. Many women dramatists have gradually and quietly started asserting their individual identities by taking up themes that centre around women and look at issues from their point of view.[8]

Kirti Jain also belongs to a tradition of women directors who have taken up themes that centre around women. However, when she decided to take up the production on Partition, she did not have any previous inclination or intention to get into gender issues. Rather, it was the Partition-related context of the play which, according to her, gave birth to the women-specific questions. She feels that her being a woman may have been the reason for her selection of the woman-related portions from the vast array of Partition literature.[9] Her play explores the gendered violence during Partition. It deals with the lives of women who are survivors and narrates their experiences of fragmented nations, homes and lives.[10]

The play on Partition is very relevant in the contemporary context too, as some of the issues which the play throws up do not remain confined just to Partition but have their relevance in contemporary times. The anti-Sikh riots of 1984 and the communal riots in Gujarat, a western Indian state, in 2002 suggest strongly that we cannot be complacent in thinking that Partition is an event that occurred in another country and belonged to a time long past. Indeed, it seems that we can hardly comprehend what is in our midst now without going back to what transpired then, excavating those memories and ransacking history. Each eruption of hostility or expression of difference swiftly recalls that bitter and divisive erosion of social relations between Hindus, Muslims and Sikhs; each episode of brutality is measured against what was experienced then. The rending of the social and emotional fabric that took place in 1947 is still far from mended. Women are the targets of violence in all such communal tensions and riots.

Addressing these issues, the play directed by Jain hinges on an interplay between the past and the present. The violence faced by women during Partition continues down to the present, as she reflects thoughtfully in the brochure to the play:

> The idea of the play is to focus on how women become targets of continuing violence by being made symbols of the family/community/nation's honour, and how they are sacrificed in the name of honour without their consent or choice. The fact that violence is perpetrated on women not just by perceived enemies but also by their own families makes for a disturbing revelation that has been repeated down the ages, whether it is the Sati, or the 1984 riots or the Partition.[11]

The play evolved through improvisation – the playing of dramatic scenes without written dialogue or a script, where the actors brought their own experiences and feelings about such trauma. In fact, the process of making a play itself is very significant from a feminist perspective. Generally placing women's experience at the centre of their practice, some women dramatists have revised the concepts of plot, character, time, place and meaning to re-create theatre. Since performance is at the heart of the structure, so within a performance situation the written text is not necessarily the definitive one. This also means experimentation with the process and form of dramatic writing. The process is open-ended, non-judgemental and provides space for divergent views and experiences. The very act of sharing experiences in the improvisation process itself becomes significant, providing meaning and a special place to the actors participating in it. There is also faith in the collective process of making theatre, as women in theatre believe that there are layers of creativity within each person and that talent has no single form.

In the first month of rehearsal for the play *Aur Kitne Tukde*, the director did not work on the script but on improvisation. This involved the employment of games and

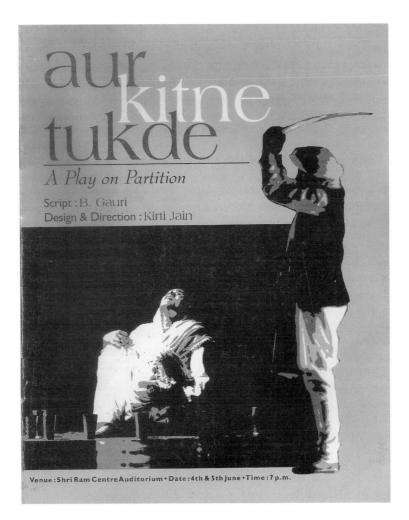

Figure 1 The front cover of the brochure for the play. Reproduced courtesy of photographer S. Tyagarajan and Natrang Pratishthan Archives.

situations centred on memory, displacement, loss, choices, childhood and others. The emphasis was on the meanings of loss – of one's family, home, country, honour, life and everything – so as to gaze at the enormity of the situation and to understand the crisis at a human level. Most of the actors were from the Punjab – the region most affected by the Partition. The actors talked to their families, relatives and friends about Partition and in the process discovered that some of their own relatives had gone through the trauma of Partition. They brought with them these experiences of their parents and relations. Hence the process became very personal and contributed to their level of involvement. A lot of the games were focused around the actors' memories of childhood, which made them connect in their own unique ways to the play. They brought the aspirations of childhood, love and marriage, and the shattering of their dreams, into this production very emotionally. A central question for the actors related to what the woman who had gone through violence during Partition would have thought at that time; taking their cue from this, the actors explored their own feelings, thoughts and reactions when confronted with such a situation. The improvisation made the actors traverse the journey of Partition. The experiences and feelings explored during this process became an integral part of the production. B. Gauri, an actor in this production who was assigned the task of writing the script, incorporated into the script the experiences that emerged during the course of improvisation.

VISIBILIZING VIOLENCE ON WOMEN

One of the stories of the play develops around Vimla, who is raped and disfigured in a horrific train journey at the time the country was divided. As a girl Vimla is carefree, spirited, loves dressing up and wants to look beautiful. However, Partition changes the whole course of her life. Vimla talks of her experience to her sister. She recalls the night that she was raped. She remembers in precise detail how, before the train reached the station, it slowed down, the lights were switched off and the window shutters were pulled down. When the train stopped at the station, voices were heard saying open the door and kill them. Vimla was seized with fear and did not know what to do. Suddenly she saw five men in front of her with swords in their hands. She struggled to hide but was gang-raped and the men cut her breasts. She exclaims: 'We were fighting for the nation's honour. For me it was not the nation that was being chopped, but it was my body. There were celebrations all over the country as the boundaries were demarcated, but those boundaries were simply symbolized and inscribed by our bodies. Our honour was being saved by taking *ours* away.'[12] When Vimla returns home, her father turns her away because, as a raped woman, she is now 'tainted'. She joins an ashram and becomes a social worker. Her job consists of recovering abducted women and restoring them to their homes.

Vimla's story serves as an instance for thousands of women who became victims of sexual violence, rape and molestation during Partition. In fact, sexual assault is the most

Figure 2 Vimla's train carriage is entered by men armed with swords. Reproduced courtesy of photographer S. Tyagarajan and Natrang Pratishthan Archives.

predictable form of violence that women of one community face from the men of the other, in an overt assertion of their identity. The woman's body and sexuality are the site of 'honour' of a community. Since time immemorial, rape has been a prominent feature of war, a conscious process of maximizing the intimidation of a conquered people.[13] During Partition, due to the heightened emotion of the situation, sexuality and power became especially commingled. This magnified the tension over ownership and 'honour' related to female sexuality, leading to terrible violence being inflicted on women of both societies. Women's bodies became a territory to be conquered, claimed or marked by the assailant.

Another story is that of Harnam Kaur, who is a survivor of a mass suicide where Sikh women killed themselves by jumping into a well – in order to escape from Muslims ravaging the village – for fear of being raped or converted to Islam. Another connected scene shows how, as news is received that Muslims have surrounded the village, the Sikh community gets together and the men decide that for the sake of the community's 'honour' the women have to be martyred. Both these scenes can be seen in the context of the incidents of March 1947, some months before Partition, that took place in a number of Sikh villages around Rawalpindi – such as Thamali, Thoa Khalsa, Doberan, Choa Khalsa, Kallar, Mator and others. Here, during an eight-day period from 6 to 13 March, much of the Sikh population was killed and houses and *gurudwaras* (Sikh temples) were destroyed. Around 5000 people were killed in the region. In one of these villages, Thoa Khalsa, some ninety women threw themselves into a well in order to preserve the 'sanctity' and 'purity' of their religion, as otherwise they would have had to face conversion.[14] Harnam Kaur's character is based on the oral narrative of Basant Kaur (a pseudonym), who survived despite her attempt to drown herself in the village well at Thoa Khalsa with the other women. She survived because there was not enough water in the well to drown them all.[15]

The play dramatizes these incidents. Harnam Kaur's scene begins with children (played by adults) playing around a slide. Suddenly they decide to enact the legendary event of women jumping into the well, which they have heard from their elders. One by one, they climb to the top of the ladder and then propel themselves down the slide with cries to God. One by one, they all die, and then it is Harnam Kaur's turn. Excitedly, she too goes up the ladder and slides down. She reaches the floor and says: 'Oh! But I did not die!' The children tease her and tell her that she did not try hard enough. She tries again, reaches the bottom and says: 'But I am still alive!' Now the taunts that come are no longer from children. The children's game gradually transforms into a world of grown-ups, with cries like 'You are a shame to our honour; you are a stain on our martyrdom'. Harnam Kaur, now a real adult, climbs the ladder and tries again to kill herself. She reaches the bottom and, startled, says: 'Again, I did not die.' There are too many bodies in the well by then and not enough water. She survives. People avoid her and even consider her shadow a bad omen. For Harnam Kaur, the women who became martyrs jumped only once but she feels that she goes through the process of jumping into the well every day and living like the dead. She is very lonely and says that to bear such loneliness one needs great strength. She remembers her daughter Mann and thinks of how she would have had grandchildren by now if she were alive.

The locale of the other scene is the mansion of Sardar Veer Singh, the village headman, who is also Harnam Kaur's husband. As news arrives of Muslims approaching, everyone in the village is asked to assemble at the mansion, including all the women and children. When they are all there, Sardar addresses them, saying that the reason for the call is that the time has come to show *izzat* ('honour') for the community and, to keep the 'honour' of the community high, the women have to be martyred. He will not allow at any cost his women and daughters to be sullied by the Muslims. It is his duty to protect the 'honour' of the women and the only way for him to do this is for the women to be martyred. He tells the women not to be unhappy but rather to be proud, as they are not dying but in that process becoming complete, and the whole country will take pride in them. Then he kills all the girls one by one, including Mann, his daughter.

These scenes in the play, as also the studies on Partition, reflect the belief that safeguarding a woman's 'honour' was an extremely powerful way of upholding male and community 'honour'. A whole new order of violence came into play that was perpetrated by men against their own kinswomen in the name of 'honour' killing. Very large numbers of women were put to death to avoid sexual violence against them, to preserve their chastity and to protect individual family and community 'honour'. The means to accomplish this end varied; when women took their own lives, they would either jump into the nearest well or set themselves ablaze, singly or in groups that could be made up of all the women in the family, the younger women, or the women and children.[16]

These events in everyday discourses on women's behaviour during Partition have assumed heroic form and the violence is valorized. The singular and extraordinary instance of doing a kinswoman to death is elevated to the rank of supreme and glorious sacrifice. In the remembrance rituals that are performed in Sikh temples every year, women's 'martyrdom' is spoken of in glowing terms as being the saviour of the 'honour'

Figure 3 The killing of girls by the village headman in the name of 'honour'. Reproduced courtesy of photographer S. Tyagarajan and Natrang Pratishthan Archives.

of their families and communities.[17] Invoking women's agency, one often hears men say with pride that 'they preferred to die'. In fact, this releases the men from any responsibility for their deaths and also puts a closure on the women's lives and on their speech.[18]

How does one read these accounts of women who took their own lives, or who 'offered' themselves up for death? The women may have consented to their own deaths, in order to preserve the 'honour' of the community. There can be an element of choice here. However, the notions of honour and shame are so deeply ingrained in society and internalized by both men and women that a death which has been forced onto a woman may quite easily be considered a 'willing sacrifice', even by the women themselves. While for some this may have been a choice, for others the decision must have been one they felt compelled to take because of the particular circumstances of the situation. The violent resolution was part of a continuum of violence that had death at the hands of their own kinsmen at one end and rape and brutalization by men of the other community at the other end.[19]

THEATRICAL RENDITION OF 'SACRIFICE' AND 'MARTYRDOM'

The production by Kirti Jain intervenes in discourses of sacrifice and martyrdom and exposes the dissonant voices intercepting hegemonic constructions of martyrdom. Jain wanted to emphasize in the production that these women did not want to die. She had in mind the highly acclaimed television film *Tamas* ('Darkness'), which is about the exodus of a Sikh and Hindu family to India, against the backdrop of riot-stricken Pakistan, at the time of Partition. The film depicts the kind of frenzy that is built up and shows the women voluntarily and unflinchingly jumping into the well for the sake of their religion. Even though this may have been a reality, Jain did not want to visualize the episode in this way. In the portrayal she did not want a verbal articulation of women's resistance. She did not want to break the reality of the truth that the women were not asked. Drawing upon this, Jain tried to show women's reactions to the choices that are made for them through the body language of the actors on stage. Theatre has that advantage of communicating resistance through the body, through expressions, silences or pauses. The question that was put in front of the actors was the need to look at what these women must have thought or gone through at the time of jumping into a well or burning themselves. Reflexivity was expected by the director from the actors through a form of method acting whereby they were encouraged to enter the minds and bodies of the women protagonists of Partition in order to gauge their feelings and reactions. According to Jain, from today's perspective heroism has no meaning and is simply planted on the Partition women. Instead, she wished to concentrate on that tiny moment before the women faced death. Jain felt that the 'choice' as yet unexpressed by these women was captured in that fleeting infinitesimal moment just before they died, when they must have stopped and thought of something which could be an exploration of fear, desire, nostalgia for someone, or something else. She wanted to see the expression on the actors' faces which seemed to say, 'Oh God, why am I doing [this], why is it happening to me?', unlike the heroic jumping that happens in *Tamas*.[20]

Jain wanted to emphasize, and the play shows this too, that when Harnam Kaur survives, her first instinct was to feel a sense of relief. In the play, as Harnam Kaur lies in the darkened well with dead bodies around her, she discloses:

> When I realized I was alive, a tiny part of me was relieved. I know it is wrong. But before understanding what is right or wrong it was the truth. My being happy was the truth. I strengthened my mind and jumped again. I failed. I remembered trivial details: the money I tried to save, my quarrel with Santosh. Had I known I was going to die, I'd have apologized to him. I jumped into the well a third time. But I still did not die.[21]

Harnam Kaur endangers herself to come to the other side (India) to save Jeet, her son, but now her son is ashamed of her. The character of Jeet draws upon the oral narrative of Bir Bahadur (pseudonym), son of Basant Kaur. Bir Bahadur, in his interview with Urvashi Butalia, refers to the incident of women jumping into the well in Thoa Khalsa and talks of one woman who despite many attempts did not die. Nowhere in his interview does he admit that the woman he speaks of is, in fact, his mother. While he dwells upon his sister's brave death at the hands of his father, he simply erases his affiliation with his mother, whose persistent presence in his life disturbs the narrative of familial 'honour' that Bir Bahadur wants to assemble.[22] Kirti Jain weaves the relationship between Harnam Kaur and Jeet into a scene. Jeet feels humiliated because his mother did not jump into the well and die when all the other women of the community did. Harnam Kaur bemoans the fact that her son carries around with him a lingering sense of his mother's betrayal and cowardice.

The scene brings out the dilemma between Jeet as a child and Jeet as an adult who looks upon the incident of 'mass massacre' differently. As a child, when Jeet witnessed the massacre scene, he felt very protective towards his mother and prayed to God to save his mother. He also felt that without his sister he would be very lonely. He was

Figure 4 Harnam Kaur praying before jumping into the well. Reproduced courtesy of photographer S. Tyagarajan and Natrang Pratishthan Archives.

even scared that his father would kill him, but to that Harnam Kaur sarcastically says: 'No son, you will not be killed. If you die who will protect the honour of women of your house?'[23]

However, as an adult Jeet is very embarrassed by his mother's survival because she could not become a martyr. He feels that he cannot walk with his head held high in front of his neighbours and also regrets his earlier action of having prayed to God to save his mother. As an adult, he feels that his father did good to save the 'honour' of the community and looks upon his sister's martyrdom with a great deal of pride. He tells his mother that he is very proud of his sister's self-sacrifice but is ashamed of her. He also stresses that for the 'honour' of the community his sister offered herself up to be a martyr, of her own choice. At that Harnam Kaur laughs bitterly and asks: 'Of one's choice!! Just as women "voluntarily" commit sati, you mean?' Harnam Kaur challenges Jeet's naive internalization of the dominant rhetoric of martyrdom: 'Are you sure your sister really wanted to die?' She wonders why her daughter's friends had quietly hidden some money and jewels before they jumped into the well. She questions the notion of women's choice in death. Her words expose the cracks in the family narrative at the same time as it exposes the celebration of 'suicide' and punctures the coherence of the master narrative in which the death/sacrifice of women was considered as 'normal'.

Many women of Hindu and Sikh communities must have seen their own men as perpetrators of violence towards them, for just as there were 'voluntary' suicides, so there were also mass murders. The feminist scholar Urvashi Butalia, in her writing on Partition, has been trying to foreground 'honour killing' in the domain of violence. According to her, the manner in which ninety women in Thoa Khalsa village in the Punjab chose to die was no less violent than, although certainly different from, the generally visible violence, that is killing and looting, that formed a part of Partition. She further adds that so patriarchal and communalized are the notions of violence that one only sees it as relating to men and the 'other', that is, the aggressor. However, 'honour' killing and other such violent acts are quite deeply ingrained in a society which erases women as 'subjects'.[24] There is a need to underscore the violence of communities with patriarchies embedded in them, which both men and women help to build and sustain.

In the play Jain draws an analogy with sati, where women are burnt alive on their husband's pyre and the act is seen as that of 'self-immolation'. It symbolizes the chaste and devoted wife able to sacrifice her life for her husband. Some Hindus believe the act of 'self-immolation' by a widow facilitated the attainment of spiritual salvation for her dead husband. Hence, the woman who commits sati is revered as a goddess in mainstream Hindu society. Feminists have been arguing that sati is a crime against women and that such acts are not voluntary but those of women being forced into 'self-immolation'.[25] Jain successfully integrates the comparative approach and compares and contrasts sati with the violence perpetrated against women during Partition.

ABDUCTED WOMEN: DIVESTED OF CHOICE

The play has two stories based on the experiences of abducted women during Partition. A large number of women were abducted during Partition and the recovery of these women was crucial to the Indian state. The families, more particularly men, brought pressure upon the state to launch recovery operations. In more 'normal' times, men would have seen themselves as the protectors of women; the fact that many of their women had been abducted meant coming to terms with an emasculation of their agency. Unequal to the task of recovery, they now had to hand it over to the state. For the post-colonial, deeply contested, fragile and vulnerable state, this was an exercise in restoring its legitimacy.[26] The governments of India and Pakistan entered into an Inter-Dominion Agreement in November 1947 to 'recover' as many women as possible, as speedily as possible, from each country and 'rehabilitate' them to their 'native' places.[27]

The stories of the abducted women in the play have been set against a background scene where the whole agreement concerning recovery is put before the assembled people by the judge and debated. Various voices give their opinion on the governmental agreement and the implementation part of it. One person asks from what date the agreement would be implemented, as the battle of Partition has not happened at the same time in all locations. A woman says that some women may have settled in new houses, taken new husbands and borne children, and therefore there was no sense in making them homeless again. Another person raises a moralist concern that abducted women may not be 'pure' (read 'chaste') as they may have gone through many hands and there was no guarantee that their families will accept them back. A countering voice questions why such women should be blamed when it was not of their own doing. Many express doubts about the families receiving their womenfolk back and treating them with respect. One woman points out that the situation of some poor women has actually improved as they are getting good food and better clothes to wear in their adopted homelands. One person asks: 'Shouldn't an abducted woman be asked of her choice?' A countering voice states that there is no need to consult the women. Amidst such voices, the proposal is passed and volunteers are asked to give their names and start the work soon.

One of the stories of the abducted women is that of Saadia. The idea of this story is taken from Jamila Hashmi's short story 'The Exile', in which a Muslim girl is abducted and forcibly married to a Hindu man.[28] The play shows that Saadia is abducted and brought into a Hindu family, where she waits for her brother to come and take her back. Saadia recalls her simple and joyful life before Partition. She describes her relationship with her brother, whom she loves dearly. She recalls how they used to play together and visit the fair together. During Partition, Raghuvir, her husband, drags her away from her home and forcibly marries her. Raghuvir and his mother, who are Hindus, on realizing that Saadia is a Muslim girl, decide to change her name. Without even consulting her, they change her name to Sumangala. She tries to protest, saying that her father had given her her name with a great deal of love, but is silenced by her husband. She hates to be addressed as 'daughter-in-law' by her mother-in-law. Saadia is hopeful that her brother will come and rescue her. However, her hope gradually fades, especially after the birth of her daughter, though she finds some solace in her love for the little one. Saadia hears the news that the police are taking those women who were abducted during the Partition back to their homes. She is very excited for she thinks that her brother will then definitely come to take her home. When the police official

Figure 5 Saadia's forcible abduction by Raghuvir. Reproduced courtesy of photographer S. Tyagarajan and Natrang Pratishthan Archives.

comes, she does not find her brother. She wonders why her brother did not come, and many doubts rise in her heart about the official – will he take her home or will he rape her on the way, will her brother accept her after so many years of living with a Hindu, and will her husband let her go, will he let her take her daughter? She makes the 'choice' not to return to her parental home, thereby ending all hope of ever going home.

Another story is about Zaahida; it is based on the well-known Zainab-Buta Singh tragedy of a Sikh husband and a Muslim wife who lived in India after Partition. This story brings out how, apart from notions of 'honour' and virtue that provided the rationale for the rescue operation, there were also material considerations. For several years after Zaahida's disappearance, the girl's relatives, mainly aunts and uncles who lived on land contiguous to that of her family, made efforts to trace her. Zaahida's uncle wanted her to marry his son, in order to keep control of the family's property, which would otherwise have been, presumably, taken over by the state.[29] The play unfolds the story of Zaahida as a teenager in love with a Muslim boy called Javed. Their teenage love does not seem to be concerned with the prospect of the division of the country. They consider Partition to be a distant possibility that may help them run away from their relatives, who do not approve of their relationship. Only when Zaahida's mother informs her that they all have to leave the village, as Partition has been finalized, do they realize that they are to be separated by this division.

During Partition Zaahida is abducted and goes through many hands. Kirtar Singh, a Sikh, brings her home and marries her. The play shows that she is happily married to Kirtar Singh. As a Muslim woman she has not renounced her faith. But Zaahida's settled and happy life with her loving husband Kirtar Singh is torn apart when the police and a social worker come to take her to Pakistan. Kirtar Singh tries in vain to explain that the whole issue is related to property and that Zaahida has a bad uncle who wants to snatch the land. Zaahida has been living with Kirtar Singh for eight years and has two daughters, and she does not want to leave, but she is taken away forcibly, as it is a legal requirement to take her to Pakistan, as per the act of Parliament passed by the government.

After a lot of effort and hardship, Kirtar Singh reaches Pakistan to retrieve Zaahida. He is presented in court, where he is asked how he is related to her. Kirtar Singh animatedly makes his case to the judge and recounts that he had to change his religion from Sikhism to Islam in order to enter Pakistan, which he readily did. He explains their relationship in great detail. He explains to the judge how Zaahida was forced to leave him despite many remonstrations. He entreats the judge: 'The creation of Hindustan means nothing to me if my Zaahida does not return to her home. I only need your signatures to take her back.'[30] Throughout this scene Zaahida remains motionless, unyielding in her silence. Kirtar Singh rushes to her and drapes her with a blue scarf – her favourite colour. When Zaahida is asked by the judge, she simply says: 'I am a married woman, I do not know this person.'[31]

The episodes of Zaahida and Kirtar Singh explore the violence perpetrated by the state in forcibly recovering women who had rehabilitated themselves in their new environment. The vocabulary of recovery, rehabilitation, homeland was actually a euphemism for returning Hindu and Sikh women to the Hindu and Sikh fold, and Muslim women to the fold of Islam. Thus even for a self-defined secular nation the natural place/homeland for women was defined in religious, indeed communal, terms. Families, communities and governments converged to 'recover' these women with extraordinary zeal and restore them to where they 'rightfully belonged'. Women's sexuality, as it had been violated by abduction, transgressed by enforced conversion and marriage and exploited by impermissible cohabitation and reproduction, was at the centre of debates around nationalist duty, honour, identity and citizenship in a secular and democratic India.[32] The whole process disregarded the interests of these abducted women, divesting them of any right to choose where they wanted to stay and with whom. It is not known how many women actually wanted to be 'rescued', how many were ready to face a second trauma, a second dislocation, and what their feelings were. Apart from a few sporadic discussions of the fate of the abducted women, most records are quite silent on the experiences of the others.

WOMEN ACTORS AS PROTAGONISTS: LOSS AND HOPE

The play highlights the violence that women suffered during Partition in the form of abduction and rape or death at the hands of their own families and often at their own hands. Women faced violence not only from others but also from their own community in the name of 'honour'. All these issues are addressed in the play by foregrounding the women in the narrative. Women are the focus of enquiry as well as agents conveying experiences in this Partition narrative. However, these are disturbed voices of anger questioning the meaning of Partition and the new nation for women. Vimla, the victim of rape in the play, explicitly critiques the problematic claim that equates national honour with female bodies. Harnam Kaur challenges the whole notion of the mainstream heroic and martyrdom discourse, demystifying the suicide episode. She questions women's choice of voluntary sacrifice, drawing an analogy with sati, where the whole event is elevated to supreme and glorious sacrifice. In the words of the director, women are the symbol of community 'honour' but they are not asked whether they want to die for 'honour' or not. This is very poignantly brought out in the last scene of the play, where Zaahida says:

> Forgive me Kirtar. But what could I do? How many times have I been divided?! In the first country I was told to wear the Salwar Kameez and not the saree. Then I was told, 'go on then and keep this man and not this one'. After which, I am ordered to go and live in this country and not in that country and now be his wife and not that of the previous one!!![33]

The play, through the voices of the four characters, makes an important intervention into the gendered violence during Partition which impacted and altered the lives of thousands of women. Despite this, the play somehow slips into reifying the image of the female victim. One would not like to argue that the predicament these women found themselves in was not traumatic or fraught with anxiety and uncertainty. But the purpose is to look beyond these at the many discordant notes and at the conflicting claims made and voices raised at the silence that was almost unfailingly imposed on women after the event. In the martyrdom and honour discourse, elements of resistance and defiance remain invisible. There have been cases of women who refused to kill themselves or their children. The recovery and restoration of abducted women to their original homes were met with spirited opposition from many of the abducted women themselves. Quite a few simply refused to return to their homes and a number of women managed to escape from the transit camps.[34] Here, the conventional focus on the victim-hood of women, while valid and deeply relevant, marginalizes other areas of experience. Besides, recent research highlights the paradoxical intertwining of great loss with new beginnings during Partition. Just as a whole generation of women was destroyed by Partition, so also Partition provided an opportunity for many to move into the public sphere, in a hitherto unprecedented way. Force of circumstance, economic necessity and the urgent need to rebuild homes and futures pushed many women of all classes into earning and supplementing family incomes. Many, had they not been pressed into public space as a consequence of Partition, would probably have led the conventional lives of women of their social and economic class.[35] Generally this 'coming out' has been hailed as a liberating experience, but one needs to problematize it too.[36]

CLIMACTIC CATHARSIS OF EMOTION

The whole production process generated an emotional response among the actors and the audiences. While working on the production several actors became aware for the first time of the dimensions of the women's suffering during Partition, even though many of them were from the Punjab, the region worst hit by Partition violence on women. The whole improvisation process of the play made them traverse the journey of Partition. One of the actors mentioned that she went through the trauma of pain and experienced death in every performance. In the interview, B. Gauri said that she had been eating, drinking and reading Partition for months. It was her greatest desire that the play be staged in Pakistan. In fact, when she landed in Pakistan for the performance, she quietly touched the Pakistani soil and kissed it. She strongly felt connected to Pakistan and had a sense of belonging to the place. She had become so emotional that when Pervez Musharraf, then President of Pakistan, visited India, she wanted to meet him to share her feelings about the futility of the division and the rift between the two countries.[37]

The play was also a huge learning experience for the director. She came to understand Partition and the issues that emerged out of it better while working on the play. She too became aware of the scale of the violence that accompanied Partition. She had not known before of the large-scale 'honour' killings of women in the Punjab by their own families. In fact she did not realize that in the close vicinity of the locality in Delhi where she had lived for so long there also lived many families from parts of the Punjab where there had been mass 'honour' killings. The knowledge of this gave her an eerie feeling. She had also not been aware that after eight years of independence an agreement was made to remove Hindu women from Pakistan and Muslim women from India without their consent. So the play for her was an exploration of the whole issue of silence around Partition. It made her understand the society better, and how society is full of 'honour' and 'shame'.[38]

The play generated compassionate responses among the audience too. They were moved by the sufferings of women during Partition. After the production, many of them came to share with the director and actors the experiences of their families and relatives who had gone through the trauma of Partition. After seeing the production, which possibly helped them to overcome the embarrassment associated with Partition events, they felt the urge to share the experiences undergone by their immediate relatives during Partition. People had come to terms with the horrors of Partition and could share their experiences because of the emotional distance from the event now. Moreover, theatre provided an important platform for sharing such experiences. The lady who was helping with the costumes in the production told Jain how her uncle had killed eighty women in her family and her mother had run away with the two children.[39] B. Gauri said that after one of the performances in Delhi a spectator came and told her that 'maybe my grandmother was a Muslim but she never told us and we never asked'.[40]

The play was also staged in Lahore in Pakistan. The audience in Pakistan was equally emotionally moved after watching the performance. One elderly lady wanted to meet the performers after the production but she was so emotionally overwhelmed that she was unable to speak. She left for home immediately, leaving a message with her daughter-in-law to tell B. Gauri that the play was very well written and performed. This elderly lady stayed in Delhi before Partition. The daughter-in-law told B. Gauri that now she could see what had happened on the other side, that is, in India. In fact, many Pakistanis said that in their history books it had not been stated that Hindu women too had suffered during Partition. There were also some responses that it was natural for Hindustan to think of Hindustani women's suffering and Pakistan to think of Pakistani women's sufferings. Many audience members also expressed their desire to come to India. They felt that the whole thing between India and Pakistan was a mere power struggle.[41]

Everywhere the play was staged, it struck an emotional chord amongst the audience. Although the director had wanted to take the play beyond the emotional to a level that permitted analysis, somehow the responses of the audiences remained confined to the emotional level and did not translate into critical consciousness. One of the important issues the director wanted to highlight through the play was the notion of 'honour' – that is, how women were killed by their own families in the name of 'honour'. The women were not asked whether they wanted to die for 'honour' or not. The women had no choice. The massacre scene in which the Sardar killed the women and girls of his own family is designed to generate a discussion on the concept of 'honour'. But the critique of the violence embedded in 'honour' killing does not come across to the audience, not even in the Punjab – the territory with a legacy of martyrdom. When this play was to be staged in the Punjab, Jain was a bit apprehensive that the Sikh audience would be angry at the massacre scene. But contrary to her expectations, the Sikh audience greatly appreciated the play. The kind of praise that Jain received made her rethink the critical angle of the play. In the massacre scene, as pointed out by her in the interview, she had made an effort to bring criticism through the voice of a little girl who does not want to be killed and is even ready to convert to Islam. Jain also tried to show that choice was available in the form of shelter being offered by a Muslim. But the tonality and the critique of 'honour' killing as desired by the director could not be communicated to the audience. The play remained an illustration of how people died and for the Sikhs it was reliving their history. Despite the overall impact of the scene, the tragedy overpowers it. After the performance, the audience told the director how the play had moved them and how they had cried a lot. Rather than making Jain particularly happy, this made her rethink her portrayal of the scene. Jain felt the need to bring in an obvious comment as to why the women were killed.[42] In this context, the analysis of Bertolt Brecht, the German playwright and director, becomes very pertinent. Brecht believed that the experience of a climactic catharsis of emotion leaves an audience complacent. For him a play should not cause the spectator to emotionally identify with the action before him or her, but should instead provoke rational self-reflection and a critical view of the actions on the stage. For this purpose, Brecht employed techniques that remind the spectator that the play is a representation of reality and not reality itself, through a distancing effect, estrangement effect or alienation effect.[43]

To understand the impact of the play one also has to understand the audience and bring it to the centre of the analysis. Many a time the spectator perceives meaning in a way different from the director – because of her/his predilections, preconceived notions and prejudices. Audiences are not homogeneous and have a subject position in the larger social structure.[44] Located in the larger patriarchal structure, audience members bring their ideological underpinnings with them to the performances. The play, while providing a vivid portrayal of the sufferings of women during Partition, gives us little or no indication of the social forces that formed it. It remains focused on an event in time – the Partition event. In the conception of the play, where improvisation played a significant role, patriarchy as an ideology and structure is not grappled with.[45] The larger question as to why women become targets of violence during Partition remains unanswered, even to the actors. Violence on women is looked upon as a manifestation of the unusual events/circumstances.[46] To understand the reasons for women being subjected to sexual violence in a communalized situation, one has to comprehend the larger patriarchal structure. Moments of rupture and extreme dislocation, extraordinary as they are, underscore the more mundane violence and abuse that form part of the everyday experiences of many women in patriarchal society. The dramatic episodes during communal riots bring to the surface, savagely and explicitly, familiar forms of sexual violence against women. In this respect, the rape and molestation of Hindu, Sikh and Muslim women before and after Partition probably followed the familiar pattern of sexual violence, and of attack, retaliation and reprisal. What is remarkable is the exultation that accompanied it. So if one does not grapple with patriarchal ideology and try to view the effect as the manifestation of patriarchal society, the circumstances and particular violence may look peculiar to a situation like Partition. It is in this context that one would like to highlight the pre-Partition life of the women depicted in the play, which evolved primarily in the improvisational phase of rehearsals. In fact, to highlight the devastating impact of Partition in particular on women, the pre-Partition lives of the women in the play are depicted as joyous. Somehow the play slips into the polemic of good days of pre-Partition times and bad days of Partition times, and glosses over the larger patriarchal structure pervading the society.

In the end, however, one cannot undermine the significance of the play, despite certain limitations. The article has addressed the silences around Partition in the cultural medium of theatre. It has also highlighted how the whole production process and the presentation of the play were an exploration of the silence around Partition for the director, actors and audience. Taking cognizance of the sexual violence during Partition is significant in a society which had long been silent on the matter because of the associated notions of embarrassment and shame. The exploration of gendered violence in the medium of theatre is also very significant because of theatre's reach into a larger audience as compared to other art forms. The article has highlighted how the play became an important facilitator and platform for people to come out of their closets and silences in order to share their experiences of Partition. The audiences' responses were complex and diverse. The play makes an important intervention into the gendered violence during Partition. Its significance lies in the contemporary context too because of the increasing communal tensions and riots that the present Indian society is confronted with. The article has tried to foreground acts like 'honour' killing in the domain of violence, which has generally remained characterized by the rhetoric of sacrifice and martyrdom. Visibilizing such violence offers a critique of the romantic and egalitarian notion of community which remains embedded in patriarchy. An effort has also been made to problematize the whole question of women's agency and choice. Lastly, the article has probed into the question of the representation of violence, which, while generating an emotional response, need not necessarily translate into critical consciousness.

ACKNOWLEDGEMENTS

I am immensely grateful to Dr Biswamoy Pati who has been the motivating force for my writing of this article. I also thank Dr Guru Rao Bapat, Dr Vineeta Bal and the participants of the conference entitled 'The Independence of India and Pakistan: Sixtieth Anniversary Reflections', held at the University of Southampton on 17–20 July 2007, for their comments.

NOTES

1. Vazira Fazila-Yacoobali, *The Long Partition and the Making of Modern South Asia, Refugees, Boundaries, Histories* (New Delhi, 2008); Yasmin Khan, *The Great Partition: The Making of India and Pakistan* (New Haven, CT, 2007); Ian Talbot (ed.), *Epicentre of Violence: Partition Voices and Memories from Amritsar* (New Delhi, 2006); Radha Kumar, *Making Peace with Partition* (New Delhi, 2005); Mushirul Hasan (ed.), *India Partitioned: The Other Face of Freedom*, 2 vols (New Delhi, 1997); Gyanendra Pandey, *Remembering Partition* (Cambridge, 2001).

2. Urvashi Butalia, *The Other Side of Silence: Voices from the Partition of India* (New Delhi, 1998); Ritu Menon and Kamla Bhasin, *Borders and Boundaries: Women in India's Partition* (New Delhi, 1998); Veena Das (ed.), *Mirrors of Violence: Communities, Riots, Survivors in South Asia* (New Delhi, 1990); Mushirul Hasan (ed.), *Inventing Boundaries: Gender, Politics and the Partition of India* (New Delhi, 2000); Jasodhara Bagchi and Subhoranjan Dasgupta, *The Trauma and the Triumph: Gender and Partition in Eastern India* (Calcutta, 2003); Gargi Chakravartty, *Coming Out of Partition: Refugee Women of Bengal* (New Delhi, 2005).

3. I have interviewed Professor Kirti Jain, the director of the play, who is also the Professor at the National School of Drama (NSD), New Delhi, and B. Gauri, an actor and also the scriptwriter of the play.

4. Alok Bhalla (ed.), *Stories about the Partition of India*, 3 vols (New Delhi, 1994); Sukrita Paul Kumar, *Narrating Partition: Texts, Interpretations, Ideas* (New Delhi, 2004); Ravikant and Tarun K. Saint (eds), *Translating Partition* (New Delhi, 2001); Jill Didur, *Unsettling Partition: Literature, Gender, Memory* (Toronto, 2007).

5. Interview with Kirti Jain, *Natrang* [Hindi Quarterly Journal of Indian Theatre], 20(18) (June 2006), p. 60.

6. Butalia, *The Other Side of Silence*; Menon and Bhasin, *Borders and Boundaries*.

7. Jacob Srampickal, *Voice to the Voiceless: The Power of the People's Theatre in India* (Manohar, New Delhi, 1994).

8. Some examples of feminist theatre practitioners are Tripurari Sharma (Allarippu), A. Mangai (Chennai) and Anuradha Kapur (NSD). Some examples of feminist theatre groups are 'Voicing Silence' in Chennai, 'Niraksha' and 'Abhinetri' in Kerala and 'Moirana Parva' in Manipur, and some examples of women's groups using theatre are 'Saheli' in Delhi, 'Vimochana' in Bangalore and 'Vanangana' in Uttar Pradesh.

9. Interview with Kirti Jain, *Natrang*, p. 60.

10. B. Gauri, '*Aur Kitne Tukde*', *Natrang*, 20(18) (2006), pp. 10–20.

11. Director's Note, brochure for *Aur Kitne Tukde* (New Delhi, 2001).

12. The play '*Aur Kitne Tukde*', *Natrang*, 20(18) (2006), p. 14.

13. Susan Brownmiller, *Against Our Will: Men, Women and Rape* (Toronto, 1975), p. 34.

14. Urvashi Butalia, 'Community, State and Gender: On Women's Agency during Partition', *Economic and Political Weekly*, XXVIII(17) (24 April 1993), pp. WS 14–15.

15. Butalia, *The Other Side of Silence*, p. 45.

16. Menon and Bhasin, *Borders and Boundaries*, pp. 31–64.
17. Butalia, 'Community, State and Gender', p. WS 14.
18. Menon and Bhasin, *Borders and Boundaries*, p. 60.
19. Ibid., pp. 45–6.
20. Personal interview with Kirti Jain conducted on 18 June 2007.
21. The play *'Aur Kitne Tukde'*, *Natrang*, p. 14.
22. Butalia, *The Other Side of Silence*, pp. 207–25.
23. The play *'Aur Kitne Tukde'*, *Natrang,* p 18.
24. Butalia, 'Community, State and Gender', pp. WS 15–16.
25. Andrea Major (ed.), *Sati: A Historical Anthology* (New Delhi, 2007).
26. Butalia, 'Community, State and Gender', pp. WS 16–18.
27. Kirpal Singh (ed.), *Partition of Punjab 1947: India and Pakistan* (New Delhi, 1991), p. 572.
28. Jamila Hashmi, 'The Exile', in Alok Bhalla (ed.), *Stories about the Partition of India* (New Delhi, 1994).
29. Butalia, 'Community, State and Gender', pp. WS 21–2.
30. The play *'Aur Kitne Tukde'*, *Natrang*, p. 19.
31. The play *'Aur Kitne Tukde'*, *Natrang*, p. 20.
32. Menon and Bhasin, *Borders and Boundaries*, p. 20.
33. The play *'Aur Kitne Tukde'*, *Natrang*, p. 20.
34. Anis Kidwai, *Azadi Ki Chaon Mein* [In the shadow of freedom] (New Delhi, 1990); Menon and Bhasin, *Borders and Boundaries,* pp. 54–103.
35. Karuna Chanana, 'Partition and Family Strategies: Gender, Educational Linkages among Punjabi Women in Delhi', *Economic and Political Weekly*, XXVIII(17) (24 April 1993); Bagchi and Dasgupta, *The Trauma and the Triumph*; Chakravartty, *Coming Out of Partition.*
36. Rachel Weber, 'Re(creating) the Home: Women's Role in the Development of Refugee Colonies in South Calcutta', *Indian Journal of Gender Studies*, 2(2) (1995), pp. 195–210; Menon and Bhasin, *Borders and Boundaries*, pp. 192 –201.
37. Personal interview with Kirti Jain; personal interview with B. Gauri, conducted on 30 April 2007; personal interview with Harvinder Kaur, actor, conducted on 28 March 2008.
38. Personal interview with Kirti Jain.
39. Personal interview with Kirti Jain.
40. Personal interview with B. Gauri.
41. Personal interviews with B. Gauri and Harvinder Kaur.
42. Personal interview with Kirti Jain.
43. Peter Thomson and Glendyr Sacks (eds), *The Cambridge Companion to Brecht* (Cambridge, 1994).
44. Eugenio Barba and Nicola Savarese, *A Dictionary of Theatre Anthropology* (London, 2004).
45. Interview with Kirti Jain, *Natrang*, 20(18) (June 2006), p. 61.
46. Personal interview with Harvinder Kaur.

NEGOTIATING THE PAST

JOURNEY THROUGH MUSLIM WOMEN'S EXPERIENCE OF PARTITION AND RESETTLEMENT IN PAKISTAN

Pippa Virdee
De Montfort University, Leicester

ABSTRACT   In the history of Partition women have been long overlooked, often forced to hide in the shadows of their male counterparts. There are now a number of key works that have focused on the role of women, but these have largely focused on women's experiences in India. Sixty years on and we know little about Muslim women and their experiences of migration and resettlement in West Punjab, Pakistan. In an attempt to trace the experiences of the Muslim women, this article will explore their history by examining official documents, newspaper accounts and women's own testimonies. It attempts to understand how this silent history is documented from these various sources.

Keywords: Partition, Muslim women, abduction, refugee, rehabilitation, West Punjab

INTRODUCTION

The study of Partition has for a long time neglected the experiences of the masses and, more specifically, women, who have often been forced to hide in the shadows of their male counterparts. Since the 1990s first-hand accounts have been used to uncover a gendered dimension of Partition. Fiction, memoirs and autobiographical writing have further enhanced our understanding of this neglected area, often filling in the gaps left by official history. Yet, sixty years on little is known about Muslim women and their experiences of migration and resettlement during the Partition of the Punjab. Most of the new history from below has focused on the Indian rather than the Pakistan experience. In an attempt to rectify this disparity, this research focuses on women in West Punjab and their journey of migration and resettlement in Pakistan.

During the past fifteen years feminist writers and social activists such as Urvashi Butalia, Ritu Menon and Kamala Bhasin have done much to highlight the plight of women during Partition.[1] They have uncovered these 'hidden histories' and brought them into the public realm of discussion and debate. Their studies have challenged the conventional histories, which marginalized women and other subaltern groups. Much of this work, however, has been confined to Indian women and comparatively little has been written about women in Pakistan. Nighat Said Khan, a Lahore-based activist, has conducted some research, largely in Sind, but even this is not in the public domain and

Address for correspondence: Pippa Virdee, Department of Historical and Social Sciences, De Montfort University, The Gateway, Leicester, LE1 9BH, UK. E-mail: pvirdee@dmu.ac.uk

Cultural and Social History, Volume 6, Issue 4, pp. 467–484 © The Social History Society 2009
DOI 10.2752/147800409X466290

remains a largely private archive.[2] Farrukh Khan has also done some research examining Muslim women's experiences through the lens of film and literature.[3] Finally, some work has been undertaken by the Sustainable Development Policy Institute, but this has been peripheral to its wider agenda of examining issues relating to the empowerment of women and documenting their plight in contemporary Pakistan.[4]

This article attempts to narrate the journey of Muslim women from India to Pakistani Punjab through the different layers of experiences mediated by the sources currently available. Firstly, the process of abducted Muslim women's recovery will be examined to understand how official history has documented this issue. Secondly, through newspapers an attempt will be made to uncover the history of women during the early stages of the relief and rehabilitation of refugees. The examination views women not just as victims but also as positive agents who contributed to the national healing process. Finally, some of the key themes which emerged out of women's own testimonies will be examined in order to understand the longer term repercussions and legacies of Partition.[5] This narrative highlights many of the methodological issues and limitations associated with attempting to unearth a gendered perspective of Partition in a largely patriarchal society. The research is therefore just the beginning of a journey that follows these silenced voices and attempts to trace Muslim women's experience of Partition.

RECOVERING ABDUCTED WOMEN: THE OFFICIAL RESPONSE

This study begins with the state's response to one of the worst crimes committed during the Partition of the Punjab. Women were targeted as they represented the 'honour' of the family, and during these chaotic and harrowing days many women were raped, mutilated and killed, while others felt compelled to commit suicide or 'martyr' themselves in order to preserve the family honour. It is estimated that around 75,000 women were raped and abducted during this time. The official response to the issue of abducted women was to locate them and repatriate them to their former homes. The Ministry for Refugees and Rehabilitation was largely concerned with numbers; this is apparent in the fortnightly reports that record the number of women that were found and exchanged between India and Pakistan. This was a rather impersonal and statistical approach adopted by both countries, and consequently we know little about the details of the personal tragedies behind these numbers. The documents do not contain their individual accounts and they do not provide any information about the lives that were torn apart in the process. Moreover, the documentation process finishes once the women have been recovered. But what happened to them when they returned to their families? Indeed, there is a question mark over how many were actually accepted back into their families. These issues are not dealt with and thus remain hidden from the official representation of Partition and its true cost.

When the independence celebrations were taking place in Karachi and New Delhi on 14 and 15 August 1947 respectively, the regions of the Punjab and, to a lesser extent, Bengal were enveloped in scenes of mass violence, murder and uprooting. What followed was one of the largest migrations of the twentieth century. An estimated twelve to fourteen million people crossed the borders between India and Pakistan. This was the net result of the political leadership being unable to reconcile their differences during the closing days of imperial rule in India. 'Official' history has emphasized the achievement of independence, but not its human cost arising from Partition. This has emerged in later discourses.[6] There is also now a growing awareness of its gendered and class dimensions.[7] This has brought out not only the differential migrant experiences, but also the conflicts between the state and individuals. It is now established, for example, that the process of state construction and legitimization involved the forcible repatriation of abducted female migrants.[8]

The communal violence which quickly spread throughout the region had taken everyone by surprise, even though the riots in Calcutta following Direct Action Day in 1946 and in Rawalpindi in March 1947 should have prompted the authorities into taking precautions and pre-empting the ensuing violence. There is now also evidence that forms of organized and pre-planned violence and cases of ethnic cleansing took place during the frenzy of Partition, though this remains a contested and controversial discourse.[9] It is much easier to accept and justify independence and the creation of two free nations than to recall the heavy human cost at which this came. During the frenzied months of August and September it was women who bore the brunt of the most horrific crimes, leading to what could be described as forms of femicide.[10] There are first-hand accounts of abductions, mass honour killings, women's bodies being mutilated and violated, indescribable crimes aimed at inflicting pain on the 'other'. These accounts have largely remained buried under the burden of prioritizing the immediate needs of the nation and recovering the 'honour' (*izzat*) of the nation.

The dislocation was at its peak in the Punjab between August and December 1947. It was estimated by the Indian government that, by June 1948, 5.5 million non-Muslims and 5.8 million Muslims had crossed the border of the Punjab.[11] Despite the warning signs of violence-related migration in Noakhali (October 1946), Bihar (November 1947) and the Punjab (March 1947), neither the Indian nor the Pakistan governments really anticipated the mass migration. Until September 1947 the governments were unable to accept the reality that a mass transfer of population was necessary. It was only on 7 September 1947, at the Emergency Committee meeting between India and Pakistan, that the movement of people was noted as the first priority.[12] Both governments vowed to cooperate and to use all available resources to provide safety for migrants.

The ineffectual Punjab Boundary Force, which consisted of Indian and Pakistani troops under a British Commander, Major General Rees, was quickly wound up at the end of October 1947. In its place the Punjab governments set up the Liaison Agency to oversee the evacuation of refugees, which was headed jointly by two Chief Liaison Officers (henceforth CLO) based in Lahore and Amritsar. Each district also had a District Liaison Officer (henceforth DLO) who relayed information to the CLO about ground activities relating to the status of refugees and evacuation plans. This agency was responsible, along with the Military Evacuation Organization (henceforth MEO), for the movement of people across the borders of the Punjab. The CLO determined the priorities for the movement of evacuees, based on the reports provided by the district officers working in the field, in consultation with a priority board.[13] By 26 November 1947 the MEOs task of evacuating people was nearly complete, with the exception of some pockets of people in remote areas, abducted women, converted people and scheduled caste refugees who still required their assistance.[14] In the course of three months nearly six million people had been evacuated, the majority of them travelling on foot in human convoys (*khalifas*).[15]

It is worth noting that the first time the governments of India and Pakistan decided to formally address the issue of women was 6 December 1947, nearly four months after independence. It only gradually became apparent that large numbers of women and children had been left behind on both sides. An inter-Dominion conference was therefore called for 6 December, where it was decided that the 'work of rescuing these women and children and also evacuating converts from "pockets" should be carried out in right earnest'.[16] At the inter-Dominion conference the two nations agreed on a treaty; it required every effort 'to recover and restore abducted women and children within the shortest time possible' and was further stipulated that 'conversion by persons abducted after 1st March, 1947, will not be recognized, and all such persons must be restored to their respective Dominions. The wishes of the persons concerned are irrelevant. Consequently, no statements of such persons should be recorded before magistrates.' The primary responsibility for the recovery of the abducted women lay with the local police; however, MEOs, DLOs and social workers were also working closely in this operation.[17] The governments of India and Pakistan were therefore quite clear regarding their objectives of recovering and restoring abducted women as soon as possible, even to the extent that the individual views of the women became 'irrelevant' in this quest.

Following this meeting, an agreement was reached with the government of India for the promulgation of an ordinance to simplify the work of the recovery of abducted persons. The government of India had put forward the Recovery of Abducted Persons Ordinance, 1949. The government of Pakistan followed its lead. The draft ordinance ensured:

1. the establishment of camps for abducted persons;
2. the taking into custody of abducted persons by police officers;
3. the maintenance of discipline in camps;
4. the setting up of tribunals to determine whether a person detained is an abducted person or not;
5. the handing over of abducted persons; and
6. the termination of all proceedings for the production of any abducted person pending before a High Court or Magistrate at the commencement of the Ordinance and the preventing of courts from questioning the detention of persons abducted.[18]

It is important to note that the interpretation of 'abducted person' meant a 'male child under the age of sixteen years or female of whatever age who is or immediately before the 1st day of March, 1947 was a Muslim and who, on or after that, has become separated from his or her family and is found to be living with or under the control of a non-Muslim individual or family'.[19] This was an affirmation that women of any age were deemed to be abductees and therefore required the state to intervene on their behalf, whereas any male aged sixteen and above was considered responsible enough to make his own decision. The centuries-old prejudice or perception of a woman as a 'non-person' seeps through clearly in the state's view of womanhood and, as we shall see later, determines the outcomes for women's lives later.

The inter-Dominion conference also outlined the agenda for the repatriation of women to their 'rightful' homes. This involved the complex network of DLOs working with the local police, social workers and informants to locate and return women and children. As a result, Muslim women found in Indian Punjab were returned to Pakistan and Hindu/Sikh women in Pakistan were returned to India. Butalia makes an interesting point that 'even for a self-defined secular nation [India] the natural place/homeland for women was defined in religious, indeed communal terms, thereby pointing to a dissonance/disjunction between its professedly secular rhetoric ... and its actively communal identification of women'.[20] More recently, Amartya Sen has been critical of the construction of these essentialized or, as Sen refers to them, 'solitarist' identities which negate the pluralities of individual identity and a common shared history.[21] Yet this is exactly how these women were defined, primarily by their religious identity. It was of paramount importance to the new nations that these women should be rescued, rehabilitated and returned to their rightful homes.

There were many appeals in the local media to rescue abducted women in India and Pakistan, including this one published in the *Pakistan Times* on 23 December 1947:

> An Inter-Dominion Conference was recently held in Lahore to consider the best method for accelerating the recovery of abducted women. The Conference felt that a good deal of selfless work had been done in recovering abducted persons but the time had now come to make an all-out effort to achieve the maximum results in the shortest time possible. No civilisation can ignore with impunity the sanctity attaching to a woman's person. It has already been declared by both the Governments that forcible conversions and marriages will not be recognised. The Governments of the Dominions of India and Pakistan have accordingly expressed their firm resolve to leave no stone unturned in rescuing the abducted persons and restoring them to their homes. 'Above all, the doubts and suspicions haunting these persons regarding the nature of the reception awaiting them in their homes must be categorically removed. The public leaders in both the Dominions have declared that these unfortunate victims of communal frenzy must be received with open arms. Every effort should, therefore, be made to erase their unfortunate experiences and give them happy homes.' But more than that it will close a tragic chapter in the history of the recent disturbances.[22]

The newspaper article raises a number of issues which were the impetus behind this appeal and indeed the need for both India and Pakistan to rescue and return abducted women and children. Firstly, the issue of women's sanctity is highlighted in the article. This denotes that women are viewed as something more than ordinary individuals; they symbolize something that is sacred to the people. The idea of a woman's honour is inextricably linked with this concept of inviolability and chastity. Thus it was of vital importance that every effort be made in order to address and resolve the issue of abducted women. Secondly, the article highlights the need for firm resolve in rescuing and returning these women to their rightful homes. Why was it so important? Part of the answer clearly lies in the previous point, regarding the sanctity attached to women in what was at the time and still is a predominantly patriarchal society. In order to legitimate the newly acquired freedom, there was a need for the state to assert its authority, and one way of doing this was to assume the paternal role. This protective shield is only extended to those considered weak and vulnerable (women and children in this case), thereby also reinforcing the masculine nature of the state. Thirdly, there is an acknowledgement that these women may not be accepted back; it is therefore stated that it is the duty of every citizen to accept them back. This presented a huge dilemma for the state; on the one hand, it had to assert its authority and take a stance on this issue but, on the other hand, it was also compelled to deal with 'dishonoured' women. The work of the Ministry, however, extended to ten years, during the course of which the circumstances of many of the affected families changed. The idea that families would openly take back these 'dishonoured' women was simply too optimistic, and so the task of simply seizing and returning women to their homes became much more complex than had been anticipated. It has been suggested that Muslim women were more easily accepted back into their families; however, this is difficult to say because notions of 'honour' (*izzat*) were prevalent in mainstream Punjabi society and indeed are still prevalent in Pakistani society today.[23]

Finally, it is interesting that the need to close the chapter on this tragic event rests with the rescuing and return of women. Again, we can go back to the point about the sanctity of women and what they symbolized. On 17 December 1947 the drive to recover abducted women had again been the subject of reporting in the press:

> In order to ensure that the peace, which is slowly but surely returning, be made permanent, it is imperative that these unfortunate women be restored forthwith to their own people. As long as this is not done, real peace cannot return. We can reconcile ourselves to the loss of everything except honour and when our womenfolk are forcibly taken away from us, not only do they lose their honour, but we also, to whom they are related, lose it. Therefore it is but natural that we harbour ill-will towards the abductors. For the sake of good relations between Pakistan and India, this can be done by the restoration of abducted women. Let them make amends, as far as possible, for their past misdeeds.[24]

It was therefore imperative that these abducted women were returned to their own people, symbolizing the restoration not only of their honour but also of the nation's honour; once this 'honour' had been restored, the two nations could then in some way go forward. Yet there is a contradiction here because this is an area veiled in silences about a dark past. How then is it possible to close a chapter without any utterances or acknowledgements concerning this bitter legacy?

The process of recovering and restoring women was tinged with paternalistic overtones. During the initial years of the exchanges that took place between India and

Pakistan women's views were not taken into consideration; however, as the years progressed, it became more difficult to forcibly repatriate these women. Such actions were being undertaken, after all, years after the event, and circumstances had inevitably changed from the time of the initial reports. A joint Fact-Finding Commission was therefore set up with the following terms of reference:

1. to assess the extent of the outstanding work of recovery in the two countries; and
2. to advise the two governments on measures to be adopted for the speedy conclusion of recovery in both the countries.[25]

By 15 August 1955, 20,695 abducted persons of Muslim origin were recovered from India and restored to Pakistan, and for the same period 9,015 non-Muslim abducted persons were recovered from Pakistan and restored to India.[26] The actual figures may never be known but eight years after the event the restoration of abducted persons was now a concluded chapter. The government of India unilaterally discontinued the work of recovery and restoration of abducted persons and allowed their Abducted Persons Act, 1949, to expire on 30 November 1957. Following this decision the government of Pakistan repealed its corresponding act, eleven years after the issue of recovering women was first discussed.[27] The tacit agreement between the states of India and Pakistan to resolve the issue of 'female recovery' and thereby reassert their patriarchal approach concludes with a lapse in the existing law. However, less explicit is the acceptance that it was increasingly difficult to convince women to uproot themselves or to forcibly repatriate them. It is therefore difficult to assess the true scale of this crime against women.

NEWSPAPER ACCOUNTS OF REFUGEE RELIEF AND REHABILITATION

One area where we witness women's agency at work is among the women who were assisting in the refugee camps and the rehabilitation of refugees. The official documentation dealing with the voluntary work at refugee camps is limited, and so the only way to really understand women's contribution is through newspaper reports and biographical accounts. Newspapers offer a rich source of information which captures the contemporary mood of the nation; they also highlight the variance between official documentation and the work actually done by women in a voluntary capacity. These newspaper reports, taken largely from the *Pakistan Times*, document the numerous appeals aimed specifically at women for them to assist in the rebuilding of the nation. As the *Pakistan Times* was reporting in English, the readership was limited to the educated classes, but of course it was exactly these women who were most likely to mobilize local initiatives to help in the relief and rehabilitation of refugees. It is also worth highlighting that at the time Faiz Ahmed Faiz, a member of the Progressive Writers' Movement, was the editor-in-chief of the *Pakistan Times*, while the owner, Mian Iftikharuddin, was not only a well-known progressive and secularist but also the Minister for Refugees and Rehabilitation, West Punjab. The issue of refugees and rehabilitation is therefore covered extensively in the paper and provides ample material for research.

All over Indian and Pakistan Punjab, temporary makeshift camps were set up to deal with the mass migration that followed independence. There were 'concentration camps', like the Walton Camp in Lahore and the Kurukshetra Camp in present-day Haryana, which were focal points for the movement of people. Such camps would have been responsible for housing as many as 300,000 people at any one time.[28] The camps were home to millions of people who had become refugees overnight. For some it was a short experience before moving on and resettling elsewhere, for others it was a long, lingering and painful experience. Providing aid and shelter for such large numbers of people in makeshift arrangements had unwelcome side-effects; diseases such as cholera and dysentery were rampant in the camps and added to the misery. Moreover, far from being safe areas, refugee camps were always in danger of being attacked due to the concentration of communities.

From reading the reports in the *Pakistan Times*, it is obvious that the task of refugee rehabilitation was too great for the newly established government of Pakistan and the Muslim League to handle alone; it required combined efforts. Consequently, individuals that were most capable, such as local students, were enlisted to assist in dealing with the unfolding human tragedy. Women were also taking the initiative themselves and organizing and mobilizing other women to work and help in refugee camps. Indeed this was a crucial time for Muslim women to come out of 'seclusion' (*purdah*) and assist in the rehabilitation process. It was, no doubt, an appeal to their maternal instincts, but it was also an opportunity for women to improve and educate themselves. As the reports from the *Pakistan Times* show, girls were encouraged to aid in the relief and rehabilitation of women, and as a result the students of Islamia College for Women, Lahore, organized themselves into groups. They made daily trips to the Mayo Hospital for the distribution of clothes to sick refugees and were also involved in writing letters or broadcasting messages for the illiterate. In a press note released by the Ministry of Refugees and Rehabilitation, it was stated that 'so far they have delivered 1,200 clothes to the refugees in the hospital and written hundreds of messages'.[29] In addition to this, the college also opened classes for knitting and sewing, with all members of staff and students involved in this voluntary work; they devoted forty minutes of their time every day to knitting jerseys and sweaters. The college, in a further effort to aid the rehabilitation of girls, decided to admit refugee students free of tuition fees and also provided free board in their hostel.[30]

Due to the horrific Partition-related violence, medical services were stretched to the limit dealing with the wounded and maimed women and children. The lack of fully trained support exacerbated this desperate situation. Soon after Partition there was an appeal by Fatima Jinnah, who had formed the Women's Relief Committee, 'to Muslim nurses and Muslim girls and women trained in first aid to offer their services for the noble cause of saving the lives of hundreds of their unfortunate sisters'.[31] Those willing to do this work were instructed to contact the Women's section of the Muslim League. Interestingly, some of the initiatives took place before the official response by the state authorities, again emphasizing how people often used their own networks to mobilize support and provide aid for refugees.

One of the earliest initiatives was the establishment in 1948 of the Pakistan Voluntary Service (henceforth PVS) in Lahore, formed under the guidance of Begum Liaquat Ali Khan,[32] Miss Macqueen, Begum Shah Nawaz[33] and Fatima Jinnah.[34] Begum Ra'ana Liaquat Ali Khan was the wife of the first prime minister of Pakistan and assumed a leading role in the women's voluntary service. The organization encouraged women to take up responsibilities such as the administration of first aid, the distribution of food and clothing and dealing with health problems and epidemics, but voluntary help also took the form of providing the refugees with much-needed moral and emotional support. Begum Shah Nawaz, a leading Muslim League figure and member of the Constituent Assembly, made an appeal for women in West Punjab to come forward and to work for the noble cause as she saw it. In a statement on 23 September 1947 she said:

> Their mangled bodies, their tear-filled eyes and their trembling hands await whatever succour and hope we can give them. At this hour, it is the duty of every Pakistani man, woman and child to do his or her duty. My sisters, you have never failed your nation. When patriotism called, you came forth in thousands and did not hesitate to face lathi, tear-gas and bullets and some of you went to jail. Today your country needs you as never before … You are the real soldiers of Pakistan. Your motherland needs you. Your helpless sisters await your aid. You have never failed your nation before, [and] I know that you will not fail now.[35]

Initially there was a good response to this appeal and hundreds of women offered their voluntary services to the PVS regardless of the problems with transport and logistics which hampered the relief process. Begum Shah Nawaz, who was a special assistant in Rehabilitation and Employment, was keen to maintain the momentum and appealed to every woman to register her name in the women's voluntary service register.[36] However, a week later there is a report in the newspaper noting the lack of women who were willing to come forward and volunteer:

> Many women who stayed back from enrolling their names did so because they felt they were not sufficiently educated. It will surprise them to find that the kind of help needed in the refugee camps and hospitals is what most of us are competent to render. To comb a dusty head with wounds and blood clots, to wash faces smeared with dirt and tears, to soothe the nerves of an old woman broken in body and spirit both – to comfort a young mother who has been tossed off this side of the shore to face an uncertain destiny at the hands of the strangers – these are activities for which any woman is trained, and while rendering them, she will be educating herself further.[37]

Seeing the lack of volunteers, the media were quick to send out reassurances to women that their natural virtues of womanhood and qualities of womanliness, such as nurturing and serving, were enough to make them good helpers in the refugee repatriation programmes. There are many accounts and reports of Fatima Jinnah visiting camps, not only to boost morale but also to highlight the important work being done by individuals on a daily basis. This served as a further incentive for more women to become involved in the rehabilitation of refugees. On one such visit, the *Pakistan Times* of 30 October 1947 reported:

Miss Jinnah, who was shown round a number of refugees, in particular to stranded women and girls recovered from non-Muslims. She expressed her deep sympathy with them in their suffering. There were a number of lady volunteer workers busy helping the refugees in the camps. Miss Jinnah appreciated their work. Begum Azin Ullah is in charge of these workers. She explained that there is a batch of 60 workers who work in two shifts.[38]

In October 1947 the West Punjab government opened an 'Industrial Home for Mohajir widows and destitute women of middle classes to give them industrial training, which would enable them to earn an independent living in due course'.[39] The training provided ranged from work skills such as tailoring, embroidery and spinning and weaving, to the more immediate concerns of the nation such as elementary nursing and first aid, but also provided for religious instruction.[40] Trainees were given free board and lodging but with the hope that they would eventually become self-sufficient once they started earning money. Employment Exchanges were set up in order to find suitable positions for women. Other social services were also available; notably, marriage bureaus were set up where the names of girls and boys of marriageable age were entered in order to find them suitable partners.[41] Lahore was the main hub of activities, where homes for destitute women, such as the Sir Ganga Ram Widows' Home, and also a Girls Training College were established. Women rescued from East Punjab were brought to homes such as these if no relatives could be traced.

The women who were at the forefront of these activities were predominantly from elite backgrounds; they were articulate and able to organize and generate support for the assistance of refugees. We therefore repeatedly see the names of women such as Fatima Jinnah, Begum Liaquat Ali Khan, Miss Macqueen and Begum Mumtaz Shah Nawaz being reported as taking a leading role. While it was essential to have this strong female leadership, more practical and urgent assistance was also required in the form of collecting bedding, blankets (*razais*) and warm clothing before the onset of winter. On 20 December there was yet another public appeal: 'Help is required from every one especially women. I mention women, because after all they are the managers of the household. Winter clothes help should primarily be their concern. Let the women of Pakistan prove that they are good managers.'[42] There are also recommendations for 'every housewife' to follow, which would greatly benefit the 'cause of humanity'. The advice is simple:

> Why not organise a knitting competition in your mohalla [local area] or your town? Young girls would love to show their prowess, and every week there would be a fair collection of knitted garments to send to the refugee relief centres. These are some of the things which women can do to help in this great task before the country. Remember, each garment you give will save a human life.[43]

What these newspaper reports show is the active role of women in the rehabilitation of refugees in Pakistan. They were integral to ensuring that the refugees had some support and assistance when they arrived in camps. Women provided help in camps, medical care, domestic aid and education, or simply donated warm clothing for the refugees. This enabled women to become helpful agents in the creation of the new state and saw an increasing number of women come out of 'seclusion' (*purdah*) to assume a greater role in society. Yet ultimately this role had a limited impact on the empowerment of women and did not result in any radical change in their position in society.

RECOVERING MUSLIM FEMALE AGENCY: PERSONAL REFLECTIONS

Turning the focus to the women themselves, one of the issues that became apparent when conducting interviews with women in Pakistan was not just that their voices were absent from the history pages, but that they themselves felt that their voice did not matter. This was starkly highlighted during an interview that took place in Lahore. Fatima Bibi was from a relatively deprived background and living in a densely populated building.[44] We got to the top of the building and were warmly greeted. She had migrated from the nearby Wagah border area. Fatima Bibi was reluctant to talk, partly, it appears, because her brother was present at the interview and partly because she felt his views were more important than hers. When I asked Fatima Bibi about how she found out about the disturbances, her brother mumbled in the background: 'Well, now I don't have permission to talk, otherwise I could have explained everything.' I responded by saying that I just wanted to record women's experience and wanted them to explain things in their own way. Fatima Bibi said: 'What can I say? I don't recall anything.' Consequently, the brother went on to explain what had happened and what had prompted them to leave. His explanation included political analysis of the disturbances, which was most likely informed retrospectively and through informal discussions. Throughout the interview Fatima's brother remained present, sometimes remaining silent and sometimes contributing to the interview. He tried to take over not, it seems, because he did not want his sister to talk to me, but because he thought he had more knowledge and therefore a discussion with him would be more beneficial to my research. From his point of view he was assisting me in providing an informed opinion, much more than his sister could. However, the interview highlighted the ways in which women's voices have become marginalized to the extent that they have become totally silent. This case highlighted one of the problems with trying to interview women, especially illiterate women and those in rural areas. Paradoxically it is often the women themselves who have been conditioned to feel they have little of value to contribute to society.

In another interview, with Rehmat Bibi, the issue of being inferior cropped up again. Rehmat Bibi shows how women perceive themselves as being confined within the 'four walls' of their homes and how their political awareness is viewed as being lesser than that of their male counterparts. When asked about why the Partition riots took place, she replied:

> I don't know much about it, being a woman I was confined to the walls of my house; whereas, my husband was fully aware of the whole scenario. Being a political leader he also participated in announcement campaigns on rickshaws and *tongas* (horse cart) around the city during the Partition. He was awarded a gold medal by Nawaz Sharif

for his political participation in the Pakistan Movement. [What was the opinion of the general public about the Partition and the riots?] My husband knows more about it, I don't know much.[45]

Rehmat Bibi is aware that her husband was politically active and quite possibly has knowledge about these issues herself from informal discussions in the home, but she was still inclined to respond with 'I don't know much'. These constant references to the male as the person who is more informed than the female can in part be explained by the lack of education and self-esteem. Most of these women have little or no access to formal education, which compounds their inferior status within a largely patriarchal society. Their experiences are confined to the 'four walls' of their homes and they have little interaction outside that environment.[46] Farkhanda Lodi also highlighted this issue:

> Our women were illiterate and uneducated. Generally they were not allowed to go out. So they were used to living indoors. In UP [United Provinces] the women from well-off families used to go out in *dolis* [palanquin]. They were not allowed to go out without taking a *mehram* [a close male family member].[47]

Education for girls during the 1940s was still largely limited to middle-class families; amongst the lower classes it was still not considered appropriate.[48] Although education provided many with more political awareness, it is important to note that in the case of Suraya Begum, who was from an affluent background, her lack of formal education did not detract from her overall awareness of the politics surrounding the Muslim League and the demands for a separate state. Her family was well connected and politically active and while she was not discouraged from studying, she chose not to because of her own lack of interest. However, she was very astute and picked up the debates and issues from her family members.[49]

> My father then joined the Khilafat Movement and he was advocating *sooti* [homespun cotton] against imported clothes. The government offered him a good job through my paternal uncle but he was too involved with the movement's activities … Muslims were very passionate against Hindus but they fought for the independence together. During the German war, they asked the British that they will fight only on one condition that they will have to give them independence. One of my nephews went to the war as a Major. So many people from Punjab were killed in that war.[50]

However, as Farkhanda Lodi highlights, there are silences that still exist around talking about women and the horrific crimes they were subjected to during the communal violence of 1947. The trauma associated with the upheaval and violence of 1947 has created a collective amnesia about the event. This has led to many having only selective recall and choosing to consciously forget their harrowing and painful memories. The abduction of young girls was like an unspoken reality, something which existed but was hardly ever talked about because of the importance of women's 'honour'. Lodi is a renowned Punjabi/Urdu writer of fiction and in some ways is able to articulate this silenced history in a more open and profound way. Yet silence is also prevalent in her family:

My *bhabi* [brother's wife] who was also my cousin [daughter of her father's sister] and her family migrated from Kapurthala. When they came here they were wounded and shattered completely. None of them was killed but they were seriously injured … Only one woman from our relatives was abducted. But she never speaks about her abduction. As you see, our respectable culture does not allow us to speak about such things. That is why she never discusses this issue. We did hear, in our childhood, that she was abducted and they brought her back, what happened to her during that time I do not know at all. Now she is an old woman, rather very old woman. She must be young that time when they abducted her.[51]

Lodi then goes on to expose the plight of women generally, blaming society and the cultural milieu for confining and keeping women in a weak and vulnerable position.

In my opinion, it is always a woman who is born to suffer. No one, a stranger nor a close one, spares her. It was not only Sikhs who did that to her. Her own people did not spare her. She is weak, helpless and vulnerable. She has been forced to remain weak. It is the training; she gets this from her parents, culture and the social environment that develop in her a pitiable pathetic soul. Our system and society do not allow her to progress. So she is in pain, for me her life is a constant misery … Even through the ages, the plight of woman never changed, though it is getting better now.[52]

The abducted woman in Lodi's family eventually settled down and now has children, and this is another reason why these memories of a traumatic past are rarely discussed. As a mechanism for dealing with this past, families have, where possible, moved on and started a new life. The memories belong to a past that has been locked away and hidden, a secret history that is deemed too sensitive to discuss openly. However, for others the inability to reconcile themselves with the past continues to haunt them, even today. Afzal Tauseef is a writer and journalist based in Lahore who escaped the horrors of Partition only because she was away at the time:

No one would have been alive in my family, had I not been at my grandmother's with my mother. It was my mother's family house in Ludhiana *zila* [district]. While my father was on training in the fort of Phillaur, where the main training centre for police officers was … Anyway, my father was there on training and my mother and I were at grandmother's house. The rest of my family, my paternal uncles, their wives, children, my paternal grandmother and all the other people who had taken shelter in that house, because it was a big house due to crises, were shot dead.[53]

This carnage and chilling experience, which left many members of her family dead, have left Tauseef puzzled and searching for the root cause that led to such a painful division. She was forced to migrate following this massacre; displaced from her ancestral land, she has not to this day come to terms with being uprooted from her home. Further, she added:

My father was so bitter about it. He opted for Baluchistan and left Punjab forever. So for me, my Punjab was my village, which then became a part of India … Living in Baluchistan made me forget Punjab and Punjabi language. But then I started rediscovering the Punjab … I was only nine years old and was too young to develop any personal opinion about such circumstances. I was just like a scared child simply following the instructions. My father was so disheartened and disappointed. He left it straightaway, saying that: 'I don't want to live in here'.[54]

Though a child at the time, the irrationality of Partition has shaped Tauseef's views, and it was only later on in life that she was able to come back and live in the Punjab. There was much bitterness in her experiences, understandably shaped by the massacre of her family, and then subsequently shaped by the new state of Pakistan. The expectations of the new state were high and millions had paid the price for the creation of Pakistan, and so the gradual deterioration of state institutions has created a class critical of the regime, a class that is trying to understand and reconcile itself to the bitter legacy of Partition that has persisted for over sixty years.

CONCLUSION

This research has tried to highlight the gaps that exist in current research around women and Partition, which until now has focused primarily on the Indian Punjab region. Conducting research in this area has presented many challenges, primarily because the official documentation is so scant. In the period that followed Partition, notions of identity were highly communalized and women became emblematic of recovering the nation's 'honour' (*izzat*). Underlying this were the patriarchal concerns of a new state, shielding and protecting women while at the same time marginalizing women's agency in favour of national priorities. Working through the official documents, one realizes that the state was only concerned with returning and exchanging women in order to achieve some sort of closure. Yet this dark episode is still too sensitive to discuss in public and remains confined to the silent histories. Trawling through the *Pakistan Times*, a different and more fascinating dimension emerges. There the agency of women is presented as a positive force; women were assisting in the relief and rehabilitation of the refugees flooding in from India. Though most accounts indicate that these were women from elite backgrounds, they nonetheless provided encouragement for other women to come out of 'seclusion' (*purdah*) and help wherever they could. These accounts also provide a useful crossover from the impersonal official documents to the personalized accounts and experiences of women working in the relief operations. They give the names and locations of women who had been recovered, with appeals to their families to come forward. What is absent from these accounts are women's own testimonies and experiences. When we examine the highly individual accounts of women through ethnographic methodology and their own experiences of Partition, a more personalized history emerges. Their memories are determined by their experiences, which are dependent on many variable factors such as class and education. Some of the women offered very lucid and provocative accounts and some, while saying very little, highlighted their subordinate status in society. This was especially the case with the women interviewed in rural locations, who were often dismissive of their own accounts. Though methodological challenges exist with oral history, these personal testimonies offer an alternative lens through which we can understand the lives and experiences of Muslim women during Partition. Indeed, they may be the only way to get an insight into this much neglected area of study.

ACKNOWLEDGEMENTS

I would like to thank the British Academy for providing the funding to enable this research to take place. I would also like to acknowledge the assistance provided by Ahmad Salim, Bilal Ahmad, Iqbal Qaiser, Tahir Kamran and Raja Adnan Razzaq.

NOTES

1. Urvashi Butalia, *The Other Side of Silence: Voices from the Partition of India* (New Delhi, 1998); Ritu Menon and Kamala Bhasin, *Borders and Boundaries: Women in India's Partition* (New Jersey, 1998).
2. Nighat Said Khan, Rubina Saigol and Afiya Shehrbano Zia, *Locating the Self: Perspectives on Women and Multiple Identities* (Lahore, 1994).
3. Farrukh Khan, 'Memory, Dis-location, Violence and Women in the Partition Literature of Pakistan and India', unpublished PhD dissertation, University of Kent at Canterbury, 2002.
4. Ahmad Salim, *Partition, Violence and Migration: The Case of Miana Gondal*, Working Paper Series No. 85 (Islamabad, 2003); Rubina Saigol, *The Partitions of Self: Mohajir Women's Sense of Identity and Nationhood*, Working Paper Series No. 77 (Islamabad, 2002).
5. The personal testimonies used in this article are part of an ongoing project on Muslim women's experiences of Partition in West Punjab. So far thirty interviews have been conducted using a combination of structured and semi-structured questionnaires; only some of these interviews have been utilized in this article. They were all primarily conducted in Punjabi and then transcribed into English. All efforts have been made to convey the intended meanings so they do not become lost in translation.
6. Some recent studies that focus on Pakistan include: Ian Talbot, *Divided Cities: Partition and Its Aftermath in Lahore and Amritsar 1947–1957* (Oxford, 2006); Pippa Virdee, 'Partition in Transition: Comparative Analysis of Migration in Ludhiana and Lyallpur', in Anjali Gera and Nandi Bhatia (eds), *Partitioned Lives: Narratives of Home, Displacement and Resettlement* (Delhi, 2007); Ilyas Chattha, 'The 1947 Violence in Sialkot', Paper presented at the British Association for South Asian Studies Conference, University of Leicester, 2008.
7. For a discussion on class, see Ravinder Kaur, 'The Last Journey: Exploring Social Class in the 1947 Partition Migration', *Economic and Political Weekly*, 41 (2006), pp. 2221–8.
8. For a discussion on forcible repatriation, see Menon and Bhasin, *Borders and Boundaries*, pp. 65–126.
9. See further Anders Bjørn Hansen, *Partition and Genocide: Manifestation of Violence in Punjab 1937–47* (Delhi, 2002); Paul Brass, 'The Partition of India and Retributive Genocide in the Punjab 1946–47: Means, Methods and Purposes', *Journal of Genocide Research*, 5(1) (2003); I. Copland, 'The Master and the Maharajas: The Sikh Princes and the East Punjab Massacres of 1947', *Modern Asian Studies*, 36(3) (2002); Government of Pakistan, *Note on the Sikh Plan* (Lahore, 1948).
10. This concept has its roots in feminist discourse, where violence is viewed as a tool of repression and male dominance. For a discussion of this, see Jill Radford and Diana E.H. Russell (eds), *Femicide: The Politics of Woman Killing* (Buckingham, 1992).

11. Ministry of Information and Broadcasting, *After Partition* (Delhi, 1948) p. 50.
12. Brig. Rajendra Singh, *The Military Evacuation Organisation 1947–48* (New Delhi, 1962), pp. 11–12.
13. Satya Rai, *Partition of the Punjab: A Study of Its effects on the Politics and Administration of the Punjab 1947–56* (Bombay, 1965) p. 78.
14. Singh, *Military Evacuation Organisation*, p. 109.
15. Weekly Reports on Refugees, 23 November 1947, Liaison Agency Files, LVII/26/45, Punjab State Archives, Chandigarh, India.
16. Taken from a report on the work done by the Ministry and the Pakistan-Punjab Refugees Council by W.V. Grigson, Secretary, Ministry of Refugees, 27 April 1948, National Documentation Centre, Islamabad (henceforth NDC).
17. Kirpal Singh, *Select Documents on Partition of Punjab – 1947* (New Delhi, 2006), pp. 572–3.
18. Promulgation of an ordinance for the recovery of abducted persons, 23 April 1949. File 84/CF/47 Ministry of Relief and Rehabilitation, NDC.
19. Government of India, Ministry of Law, 31 January 1949, Ordinance No. V of 1949: An Ordinance outlining an agreement with Pakistan for the recovery and restoration of abducted persons. File 84/CF.47, Cabinet Secretariat, Government of Pakistan. Information kindly provided by Ahmad Salim.
20. Urvashi Butalia, 'Community, State and Gender on Women's Agency during Partition', *Economic and Political Weekly,* 24 April 1993, p. WS16.
21. Amartya Sen, *Identity and Violence: The Illusion of Destiny* (Penguin, 2006).
22. *Pakistan Times*, 23 December 1947.
23. Butalia makes the point that Muslim families were more willing to take Muslim women back than Hindu ones, in part, it seems, due to different notions of purity and pollution ('Community, State and Gender', p. WS20).
24. *Pakistan Times*, 17 December 1947.
25. File 10/CF/55 XVI Cabinet Secretary. Fortnightly summary for the period ending 30 September 1955 (NDC).
26. The final figures were 20,728 Muslims and 9,032 non-Muslims. Fortnightly summary for the period ending 30 September 1955 (NDC).
27. File 11/CF/58 (5), Government of Pakistan, Ministry of Relief and Rehabilitation. Six monthly summary of the Ministry of Rehabilitation for the Cabinet for the period ending 30 September 1958 (NDC).
28. Government of India, *After Partition* (Delhi, 1948), p. 56.
29. *Pakistan Times*, 30 October 1947.
30. Ibid.
31. *Pakistan Times*, 7 September 1947.
32. In 1949 Begum Ra'ana arranged a conference for women from all over Pakistan; this resulted in the creation of the All Pakistan Women's Association. This was a voluntary and non-political organization designed to support and strengthen women socially, culturally and through the improved provision of education.
33. Begum Shah Nawaz and Begum Shaista Ikramullah were the only two women in the Pakistan Constituent Assembly and Central Legislature in 1947. Shah Nawaz was also one of the founding members of the All Pakistan Women's Association.
34. Fatima Jinnah is referred to as Madr-e-Millat – 'mother of the nation'. She played a leading role in the resettlement of refugees and was a proponent of women's emancipation, encouraging their participation in the creation of the Pakistan state.
35. *Pakistan Times*, 23 September 1947.

36. *Pakistan Times*, 1 October 1947.

37. *Pakistan Times*, 7 October 1947.

38. *Pakistan Times*, 30 October 1947.

39. *Pakistan Times*, 15 October 1947.

40. Ibid.

41. *Pakistan Times*, 11 October 1947.

42. *Pakistan Times*, 20 December 1947.

43. Ibid.

44. Interview with Fatima Bibi, Lahore, 24 April 2007.

45. Interview with Rehmat Bibi, Faisalabad, 1 December 2002.

46. This was highlighted in a number of interviews where the women talked of having few friends and domestic tasks such as going to the market were often undertaken by their mothers rather than the young girls themselves.

47. Interview with Farkhanda Lodi, Lahore, 22 April 2007.

48. For a more in-depth discussion, see further Chapter 4 on education in colonial Punjab in Dushka Saiyid, *Muslim Women of the British Punjab: From Seclusion to Politics* (Basingstoke, 1998).

49. Interview with Suraya Begum, Lahore, 19 April 2007.

50. Ibid.

51. Interview with Farkhanda Lodi.

52. Ibid.

53. Interview with Afzal Tauseef, Lahore, 22 April 2007.

54. Ibid.

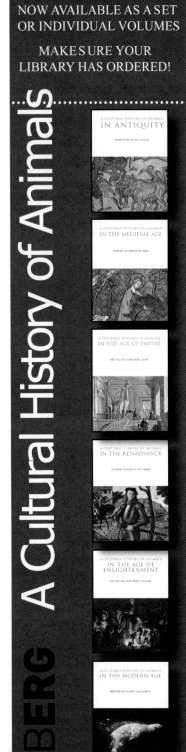

A Cultural History of Animals

Series Editors: Linda Kalof and **Brigitte Resl**

A Cultural History of Animals is a complete history of 4,500 years of human-animal interaction from ancient times to the present. Each volume presents an overview of the period and continues with essays on the position of animals in contemporary Symbolism, Hunting, Domestication, Sports and Entertainment, Science, Philosophy, and Art. Originally published as a six-volume set, each volume is now available to purchase individually.

Volume 1
A Cultural History of Animals in Antiquity
Edited by **Linda Kalof**
An extraordinarily broad assessment of animal cultures from 2500 BC to 1000 AD, describing how animals were an intrinsic part of the spiritual life of ancient society, how they were hunted, domesticated, and used for entertainment, and the roles animals played in ancient science and philosophy.

978 1 84520 361 0 • 288 pages • 47 bw illus • £60.00 $120.00

Volume 2
A Cultural History of Animals in the Medieval Age
Edited by **Brigitte Resl**
Investigates the changing roles of animals in medieval culture, economy and society in the period 1000 to 1400. During this period animals were omnipresent in medieval everyday life and there were significant changes in the scientific and philosophical approaches to animals as well as their representation in art.

978 1 84520 369 6 • 288 pages • 57 bw illus • £60.00 $120.00

Volume 3
A Cultural History of Animals in the Renaissance
Edited by **Bruce Boehrer**
Covering the period 1400 to 1600, this volume presents a broad overview of the changing role of animals in the economy, culture and thinking of the period.

978 1 84520 395 5 • 288 pages • 37 bw illus • £60.00 $120.00

Volume 4
A Cultural History of Animals in the Enlightenment
Edited by **Matthew Senior**
The period from 1600 to 1800 saw great changes in the way animals were regarded, during which the codifying and categorizing impulse of the age of reason saw sharp lines drawn between different animal species and between animals and humans.

978 1 84520 372 6 • 256 pages • 51 bw illus • £60.00 $120.00

Volume 5
A Cultural History of Animals in the Age of Empire
Edited by **Kathleen Kete**
This volume explores the cultural position of animals from 1800 to 1920 when there was a period of extraordinary social, political and economic change as the Western world rapidly industrialized and modernized.

978 1 84520 410 5 • 256 pages • 45 bw illus • £60.00 $120.00

Volume 6
A Cultural History of Animals in the Modern Age
Edited by **Randy Malamud**
Human culture is now more dangerous to non-human animals than ever before. We live in a time when the idea of an animal's habitat has almost become irrelevant, except as a historical curiosity, yet also in a time when the public and philosophical acknowledgement of animal rights and environmental ethics is on the rise.

978 1 84520 381 8 • 256 pages • 37 bw illus • £60.00 $120.00

HIEROGLYPHS AND BROKEN LINKS

REMEDIATED SCRIPT AND PARTITION EFFECTS IN PAKISTAN

Ananya Jahanara Kabir
Leeds University

ABSTRACT   This article argues for a movement away from narrative forms as a source for studying Partition and its legacy of 'Partition effects', proposing instead that Partition studies examine non-narrative forms of cultural production. It begins this task by examining the 'remediation', or visual quotation, of script within Pakistani visual art. Script – readable and unreadable – becomes a site of trauma and memorialization that reveals the affective history of post-Partition Pakistan, specifically that of Karachi and Sindh. By analysing and historicizing examples of remediated script, this article espouses a post-Partition cultural studies that privileges primary material from Pakistan over that from India.

Keywords: script, Partition, Pakistan, visual art, calligraphy

> Strange hieroglyphs of desire
>
> Kamila Shamsie, *Kartography*

> I'm fascinated by these broken links, but it is nothing to do with my life in Pakistan.
> Huma Mulji, on her artwork *Mera ghar* ('My Home')

At the close of her novel about the weight of memories and historical silences on contemporary Karachi, Pakistani author Kamila Shamsie describes an imagined encounter between the protagonist Raheen and her childhood friend turned lover Karim through an extended metaphor that collapses body and city into a single site of desire. The lovers trace 'crisscrossed paths and routes unmapped' on each other's bodies, and, at the close of the paragraph, the rain on the window blends 'roads and veins, arteries and arteries': an escalating urgency that comes to a climax with the homology between artery as a conduit for cars and artery as a conduit for blood. This conceptual and semantic blurring, facilitated by the vocabulary of urban mapping, is fully in keeping with the novel's focus on the intimate links between Karachi and post-Partition subjectivity, although it should be noted that the latter is figured here through a narrative preoccupation with 1971, the year of the war between West and East Pakistan that led to the independence of Bangladesh, rather than 1947, the year of Partition. At

Address for correspondence: Ananya Jahanara Kabir, School of English, University of Leeds, LS2 9JT, UK. E-mail: a.j.kabir@leeds.ac.uk

Cultural and Social History, Volume 6, Issue 4, pp. 485–506 © The Social History Society 2009
DOI 10.2752/147800409X466308

the same time, Shamsie's two-way metaphor gains an added suggestiveness through a third emphasis: that on language that exceeds its written form. The lovers' 'sweat smelled of unwritten words'; when finally imagined as gaining written form, these turn out to be, in the phrase I have used for my first epigraph, undecipherable 'hieroglyphs'.[1] Yet it is through this very 'strangeness' that 'desire' crystallizes. The potency of the imagined script derives here, paradoxically, from its inability to be read and understood.

This potency of the script that cannot be read reappears in an artwork by Karachi-based visual artist Huma Mulji: a poster entitled *Mera ghar* ('My Home'; see Figure 1). Designed for public display, it was part of *Aar-paar* ('Crossing Borders'), an Indo-Pak public art project.[2] This poster's running margin incorporates the phrase *mera ghar* in what Mulji claims are seventeen different scripts, representing the written forms of Karachi's various languages, including Gujarati, Kutchi, Sindhi and Urdu. This proliferation of scripts at the margins of representation visualizes the broken links that 'fascinate her', precisely because they are unreadable to her generation. When spoken, however, their versions of *mera ghar* all yield more or less the same sound and are thus comprehensible across a spectrum of linguistic communities. This oscillation between the visually incomprehensible and the aurally comprehensible makes Mulji's use of multiple scripts a resonant signifier of the complexities of home in this city of departures and migrations conducted under the fraught signs of 1947 and 1971, and in this country whose creation owes no little to accumulating tensions between the spoken sound and the written sign.[3] The post-Partition, post-Bangladesh artist's fascination with culture, here manifested in script, as 'a broken link' between an unknowable past and the lived present that it shadows is immediately rationalized as having 'nothing to do with the present'. Yet these clustered paradoxes – the links that are broken, the unreadable that can be overheard – draw tightly together that fascination with the declaration of its redundancy to a modern Pakistani.

Mulji and Shamsie are Karachi-ites from the same generation, of *muhajir* families both, albeit through different routes.[4] Both are concerned with creative expression as a means not merely to reconnect with the fact of Partition, but also to communicate the problems inherent in such attempted reconnection. One is a visual artist, the other a novelist; one uses the unreadable script as metaphor, the other visually quotes scripts that are unreadable to her. In both, the enhancing of the chosen medium of expression by referencing another medium altogether suggests a deliberate struggle, born out of desire for and fascination with what Ayesha Jalal has termed 'elseness' – something that lies beyond the 'self/other' dichotomy.[5] These two cultural producers from contemporary Pakistan thus mobilize, at least in the examples I have cited, the economy with which script, and unreadable script at that, can convey some of the most delicate and complex aspects of Pakistan's history as a 'new' nation, whose raison d'être was securing a homeland for South Asian Muslims. While the early years of Pakistan were suffused with a sense of optimism, in recent years scholarship and creative endeavours alike have turned more introspective, pausing also to consider what one recent scholar of Karachi's divided families has termed 'Partition effects, or the ways in which Partition is socially remembered and retrospectively assessed'.[6] Equally

Figure 1 Huma Mulji, *Mera ghar* ('My Home'). Reproduced courtesy of the artist.

important to our understanding of Partition effects, however, is their psychological dimension, and it is this dimension that Shamsie's 'strange hieroglyphs' and Mulji's 'broken links' help me excavate.[7]

This article examines script, both readable and unreadable, as a signifier of Partition effects within the work of Pakistani visual artists. As my opening discussion indicates, I am interested not in what script does but in what it is made to suggest within contemporary Pakistani cultural production; furthermore, I am interested in the visual aspect of script rather than what it might actually say. This suggestiveness of script has long preoccupied Pakistani modernism, most obviously in its visible, agonistic engagement with calligraphy. Contemporary Pakistani artists, engaged as they currently are in urgent debates about the contested regimes of legitimacy – cultural, political, historical and theological – that traverse the Pakistani public sphere, enter these debates by 'remediating' images of script that invite, but often resist, deciphering.[8] These remediations, or visual representations of script, cumulatively comment on how script in South Asia has borne the weight of pre-colonial hierarchies, colonial modernization, anti-colonial identity politics, and post-colonial struggles over that layered inheritance. They memorialize not necessarily specific scripts, but the *idea* of script as a charged site where language and religion, those all-powerful vectors of identity politics in South Asia, intersect. As Iftikhar Dadi has demonstrated, these references to script participate in a pan-Islamic modernism that reroutes sacralities into 'a mutilated calligraphy that *indexes textuality itself*'.[9] What I wish to focus on is the additional claim for script that such remediations make – a claim to a hermeneutics specific to Pakistan, in whose emergence and truncation the politics of script played such a crucial role. By focusing on Pakistani visual art, rather than its Indian counterpart, therefore, I offer fresh insights into the emotional significance of script within South Asia's messy partitioning of cultures, while reversing the common scholarly tendency among South Asianists to make Pakistani cultural production ancillary to a focus on India.[10] Finally, this article will move towards considering how such remediation reveals the modes of remembering and forgetting that characterize Karachi, and Sind, as 'sites of memory' for the post-1947 Pakistani subject.

DESCRIBE, DEPICT, REMEDIATE: FROM NARRATIVE TO SCRIPT, VIA THE IMAGE

The sixtieth anniversary of the Partition of India saw numerous academic and popular discussions of that event's continuing impact on history, politics and memory in South Asia. From Delhi to Karachi to Southampton, Partition's legacies were debated with an openness markedly different from the tentative forays into the difficult memorial terrain surrounding 1947 evident during the first 'significant' anniversary ten years ago.[11] There is now considerable recognition of the massive migrations, horrific violence and destruction of families, homes and cultures entailed by the division of decolonized British India into the new nations of India and Pakistan, differentiated on religious grounds. Partition studies today constitute a fruitful conversation between historians, anthropologists, literary scholars and activists collectively fighting obscurantism, inter-community stereotyping, and selective historiography in South Asia and its diasporas. Alongside academic writing, there is a proliferating production of oral histories, anthologies of survivors' recollections, and Partition-related fiction.[12] Indeed, something of a 'memorial industry' has mushroomed around the belated realization of Partition as collective trauma.[13] This cultural (re)production of traumatic memory now threatens, in fact, to congeal into a predictability that is also glimpsed within academia. The Punjab has remained the dominant focus of creative and academic responses to Partition; the discrepancies between Indian and Pakistani modes of remembering Partition, shaped by different nation-building impulses, remain relatively unexplored; Pakistan, as noted above, is examined far less than is India; there is near silence on the memorial complications caused by the independence of Bangladesh in 1971. Most crucially, I would like to contend, narrative, including oral history, novels and film, remains the favoured mode for creative practice and academic scrutiny.

By 'narrative', I mean a text or representation that possesses temporal extent and that strives to bestow on its components a relationship of cause and effect. The acts of perception and reception generate among that text's audience/readership the expectation that its temporal unfolding will be governed by a beginning, middle and end – an expectation that the text normally fulfils, although its conversion of sequentiality into narrative causality can well be complicated by co-existing non-narrative, lyric impulses. Currently absent from Partition studies is an understanding of these phenomenological complexities and their political implications. The focus of historiography, anthropological investigation and literary and cultural studies has overwhelmingly been primary materials with strong narrative components: the short story and novel, oral history, and popular cinema. Neither their embedded non-narrative moments, nor their non-narrative counterparts – theatre, music, lyric poetry, photography, painting, sculpture, public monuments – have been subjected to sustained academic scrutiny. Yet, as suggested by recent scholarship on the importance of art and music in conflict resolution, such non-narrative modes of remembering Partition enable rich new approaches to making peace with the past and present across South Asia.[14] Certain epistemological limitations of narrative also call into question its current pre-eminence within Partition studies.[15] Post-Enlightenment modes of narrative typically rely on the concept of a singular perspective from which material is organized in order to produce the linear logic of cause and effect.[16] Secondly, narrative in general privileges closure, a moment in story-telling with enormous ideological potential, in order to complete the circuit of meaning-making. Who tells the story, and whose conclusion ends it?

In the context of Partition, both these characteristics of narrative exceed their theoretical and academic dimensions. As Krishna Kumar has demonstrated, the same events during the nationalist movement leading up to 1947 are interpreted very differently within history textbooks in India and Pakistan, thanks to the divergent perspectives brought by the official grand narratives of each nation regarding Partition.[17] Likewise, as Romila Thapar has argued, narratives of Hindu–Muslim animosity of comparatively recent historical origin are read back into events in the pre-colonial past, such as the 'sacking' of the Somnath temple by Mahmud Ghaznavi, to facilitate what Simon Gikandi, in another context, calls a 'mythopoesis of history' that in turn justifies contemporary aggression against a reified 'Other'.[18] Historiography, which, after Hayden White, it is now axiomatic to consider as exemplary rather than distinct from narrative form, thus seeps into narratives of self and other, majority and minority that circulate through popular media. My contention, argued in detail elsewhere, is that this lamination, and indeed mutual contamination, of narrative modes feeds into and vitiates issues of interpretation, claim and counter-claim.[19] Excessive narrativization of Partition, I argue, mires reconciliation and understanding between collective identities both within and across nations, contributing to the continued persecution of religious minorities, the growth of religious fundamentalism, and escalating geopolitical problems in peripheral frontier zones. In the case of Pakistan, the grand narrative of the Two-Nation Theory has foreclosed the option of examining its exclusions and insistences as well as the ways in which both public debate and cultural production now far exceed its framework.[20]

With Partition studies having gained a critical mass, therefore, we need to move towards more nuanced accounts of Partition effects and to map them meaningfully on the troubled psychosocial landscape of contemporary South Asia. Diverse modes of remembering Partition – painting, photography, sculpture, public architecture, non-commercial film – have to be mobilized in order to break out of default positions of blame and guilt born out of an over-reliance on narrative modes of remembrance, and also the tendency to re-narrativize fragments of memory within acts of interpretation, embedding them within inherited prejudices that are easily mobilized as causalities. Furthermore, the increasing understanding of 1947 as a large-scale traumatic event embraced psychoanalytical concepts, particularly as utilized within Trauma studies and Holocaust studies, to enrich cumulative analysis of Partition's psychosocial impact.[21] But we have accepted somewhat uncritically psychoanalysis's reliance on models of narrative closure for the purported healing of traumatic memories, without heeding the warnings of historians of conflict who point to the susceptibility of foreclosed narratives to the enhanced sense of a group's 'chosen trauma' as the reason for its persecution of a targeted 'Other'.[22] The scope of Partition studies needs to expand by considering a range of creative media, which, by incorporating non-narrative logics, are also amenable to interpretative paradigms embedded, for instance, in 'our poetry and the Sufi gnosis'.[23] Much of the shared Indo-Pakistani cultural inheritance was visual and material: miniature painting, architecture, craft traditions, textiles. Contemporary visual art practice can quote that inheritance through form as well as content.[24] How, if at all, does it marshal those capacities into commentary on remembering, forgetting and surviving Partition? What can such art tell us about Partition that words cannot? How do visual representation's non-verbal capacities work against the biases of narrative? What indigenous modes of signification and memorialization are silently invoked thereby?

The visual or graphic field's 'hypermediacy', or its ability to quote visually other media, manifests symptoms of Partition's deep cultural and psychological impact. These symptoms are different from those the written text may evince, even though they may well yield new insights for the written text.[25] In fact, for the art project that symptomatically evokes Partition effects, writing itself radiates significance, as the opening discussion of Mulji's poster suggested. This combination of visual image and text goes beyond what has been called the 'imagetext', a 'hybrid form' that breaks down the separate semiotic regimes of texts and images, substantiating in the process post-structuralist theoretical obsessions with 'subdu[ing] the image by means of text'.[26] It is more useful to see Pakistani art's quotation of script as instances of 'remediation', where script becomes the privileged media re-mediated within the artwork.[27] Remediation here is not merely 'a repurposing, but perhaps a more complex kind of borrowing, in which one medium is itself incorporated or represented in another medium'.[28] Thus explicated, remediation emerges as the conceptual obverse of the written text that incorporates visual or graphic representation – a relationship that literary criticism defines as 'ekphrasis'. Ekphrasis denotes the verbal description of an object or painting that itself depicts some scene or event: as 'the verbal representation of graphic representation', it must 'explicitly represent representation itself'.[29] This close relationship between 'ekphrasis', whose political and aesthetic implications have been extensively theorized, and 'remediation', a term of more recent vintage, is a helpful place to begin theorizing the remediation of script in Pakistani art.

The 'perceived competition or rivalry between the new media and the old' that drives remediation can be understood better when we recall that ekphrasis too expresses similar rivalry: the 'friction' between 'pictorial stasis' and 'the fixed forms of graphic representation', on the one hand, and the 'narrative, storytelling impulse that language by its very nature seems to release and stimulate' on the other.[30] By deliberately evoking connections between the concerns of the verbal account and the contents of the visual depiction, the writer stages epistemological contests between the painting that shows and the text that tells. How does remediation complicate those contests by shifting the arena of competition to the visual medium? These politics of remediation may be unpacked by turning to the recent consensus that 'ekphrasis is always political', encoding 'the struggle for territory, a contest of rival ideologies'.[31] Thus Neil Ten Kortenaar analyses Salman Rushdie's ekphrastic description of a painting that hangs in Saleem Sinai's bedroom as symptomatic of the post-colonial attempt, both necessary and impossible, to appropriate and free oneself from the framing forces of imperialist art.[32] South Asian authors have equally used ekphrasis to comment on the impossibility of narrativizing the post-Partition traumatized self: thus Sorayya Khan's *Noor* locates the traumatic impact of the 1971 war on Pakistanis within the eponymous war-orphan, who, unable to speak, compulsively draws scenes of her life in the former East Pakistan.[33] Like ekphrasis, then, remediation is an aesthetic strategy for magnifying and commenting on the politics, history and limitations of signification. Pakistani art's remediation of script highlights not writing but *writtenness*, problematizing script itself as cultural and historical repository while acknowledging its tremendous iconic power.

FROM CALLIGRAPHY TO TYPEFACE: SCRIPT IN COLONIAL AND PAKISTANI MODERNITY

Script enters South Asian visual registers most obviously through calligraphy. As Annemarie Schimmel reminds us, 'the art of writing has played, and still plays, a very special role in the entire Islamic culture, for by the Arabic letters – heritage of all Islamic societies – the Divine Word could be preserved'.[34] Calligraphy flourished in Mughal India as an art of the book and as embellishment for public buildings; indeed, as in all Islamicate cultures, here too 'Muslim artisans seem to have covered every conceivable object with writing'.[35] Appearing alongside the most exquisite miniature paintings, on the most fragile of pottery and glassware, as well as upon the grandest of edifices, calligraphy gained both intimacy and monumentality. Being tied up with the revealed word of God, it made manifest sacral mysteries; accordingly, it had to achieve a visual beauty, elegance and intricacy that would make writing commensurate with its sacral message. Although figurative art was banned in Islamic orthopraxy, calligraphy sat in harmony with a wealth of stylized natural features as well as geometric abstraction. In Mughal India, as elsewhere in the Islamicate world, the refinement attained by calligraphy on different surfaces and within this compositional milieu made this art form a fitting repository for the sacredness of its verbal components. Even if reading these components was difficult, with the overall cast rather than legibility determining the mise-en-page, an inability to grasp the full meaning of the word heightened its mystery and majesty. Calligraphy represented 'religious emotion frozen by art'.[36]

With colonial modernity, and the dissolution of Islamicate India, the calligraphic arts declined. Compared to the 'conscious recasting of poetry for communitarian purposes in the nineteenth century', Jalal observes, 'the high Islamic arts of calligraphy and miniature painting were slower to respond to the communitarian spirit, dependent as they were on the economies of patronage'.[37] Jalal rightly critiques Benedict Anderson's thesis of print capitalism's 'imagined communities' by thoroughly examining the power of the orally communicated and enjoyed poem in colonial North India. This power notwithstanding, the typeface must be seen as a vector of modernity that ruptured older modes of cultural valorization. In the case of Urdu, the intervening technology of lithography evinced, as Robert Fraser has argued, 'a nostalgia for manuscript'; indeed, according to him, 'the South Asian lithographic revolution may well be regarded as … a radical form of print adaptation to bring it in line with traditional aesthetic requirements, even as a resistance to modernity'.[38] Nevertheless, even the seemingly less modern looking lithography could not help but push calligraphy into an unquestionably modern realm. The development of an Urdu-Persian lithographic typeface moved *nastaliq*, that most beautiful and intimate of Persian-derived scripts reserved for poetic texts, from the calligraphy of the embellished and high status manuscript into the humdrum world of printed material, including newspapers and pamphlets. Standardized and mechanically reproduced, the erstwhile 'bride of all scripts' circulated freely through a newly created public sphere, helping transform existing norms of 'linguistic diversity, multilingualism and diglossia' and convert 'linguistic repertoires' into 'languages'.[39] Standardization led, moreover, to the complex separation of Hindi and Urdu, denoted above all by two separate scripts whose mutual intelligibility was announced and reiterated by their starkly contrasting visual aspects. Not just language but script thereby became a 'multi-congruent' symbol of separate cultural and religious identity.[40] The 'sharp dichotomy between the spoken words of the many and the written scripts of the few', which Jalal draws attention to,[41] may be elaborated as the dichotomy between the slippage between registers, dialects and accents that continued in the oral sphere, and the new constrictions propagated through print.

As script moved into the demotic domain of lithographic typeface, it lost the synergy between orality and writtenness that had made calligraphy 'music for the eyes'.[42] Now, script, the print-capitalist visual expression of language, although visually looking back to the handwritten through the lithograph's particular aspect, nevertheless accrued connotations of an exhilarating modernity, while language's oral forms retained vestiges of a pre-modern sacrality that contributed to the communitarian power of oral performative expression.[43] Imperial attitudes were marked by disdain towards the 'vernacular', as Jalal has shown, thus encouraging associations of infancy and underdevelopment with oral forms of language in the Punjab. These complications to the 'transition from the identity of language to the language of identity'[44] were most pronounced in those areas where 'people continued to speak the same colloquial language in their daily interactions while the written forms were evolved to assume distinctively different appearances'.[45] Commonly associated with the United Provinces, these confusions were most heightened in the Punjab, where, as Jalal magisterially reveals, three scripts, Persian, Nagari and Gurmukhi, competed for the best fit with a slippery Urdu-Punjabi oral continuum. Depending on the script that was marshalled by religion-based identities (Hindu, Muslim or Sikh), the language purportedly changed from 'Punjabi' to 'Urdu-Punjabi' and even 'Hindi'. While 'the similarity of the spoken and the written vernacular for many Muslims in the UP… helped foster a sense of Urdu as a language of identity … in the Punjab, by contrast, the discrepancy between the spoken and the written word continued to smudge [these] narratives'.[46]

Pakistan, with the Punjab as its political centre, inherited these confusions over script and language which were constantly sought to be camouflaged through assertions of Urdu's primacy to a South Asian Muslim identity. Hence the paradox of a post-colonial nation whose state language was the mother tongue of around 7 per cent of its population, and where, defying all commonsensical understandings of hegemony, that small percentage was not congruent with the demography of the Punjab, its powerhouse.[47] Yet ideological interests and existing linguistic trends coalesced to ensure the Punjab's political supremacy. Post-colonial Pakistani Punjab continued, to paraphrase Jalal, the 'vengeance of the spoken language' already visible during the nineteenth century, when the colonial imposition of Urdu as a prestigious written language led to 'Urdu being absorbed into Punjabi dialects', rather than Punjabi's projected eradication.[48] In its spoken form, the Punjabi-Urdu continuum (along which should be situated historically related languages such as Potohari, Sindhi and Siraiki) assumed the status of a new post-colonial lingua franca, where different accents could either collapse or announce regional differences. However, this useful malleability continued to be overridden in written forms of that continuum, which perpetuated the visual impact of one script. There was, of course, one exception. If, in the Western Wing of pre-1971 Pakistan, the Persian script furnished an equivalent to the political 'One Unit', in East Pakistan, Bengali, written in a Sanskrit-derived script, continued to flourish. Offering, from Pakistan's very incipience, an impressive and increasingly threatening cultural competitor, Bengali's resilience must be at least partially attributed to its script never having been 'divided', even while the associations, from a West Pakistani viewpoint, of that script and Hinduism overrode the morphological and syntactic affiliations between Urdu and Bengali as sister languages descended from Sanskrit, and that are perceptible to the ear if not the eye.[49]

These affective and political complications of script within Pakistan must be assessed alongside the resurgence in calligraphic arts outside of print media that characterized its post-independence cultural production, and that resonated with a similar resurgence across newly decolonized Islamic nations. Not merely a reaffirmation of calligraphy's status as a pan-Islamic 'precious heirloom',[50] this phenomenon is integral to a history of post-colonial Islamic modernism, at the vanguard of which newly created Pakistan firmly placed itself.[51] This modernist and yet atavistic mobilization of calligraphy led to its redeployment, not within a new version of manuscript culture but within public monuments such as the massive *Teen talwar* ('three swords') and *Do talwar* ('two swords') adorning prominent roundabouts in Karachi's Clifton area (see Figure 2). Commissioned by Zulfiqar Ali Bhutto (1971–7), the *Teen talwar* in particular, on which is calligraphed Jinnah's dictum 'Unity, Faith, Discipline', complements and elaborates the minimalist austerity of earlier, post-independence public monuments such as Jinnah's Mausoleum at Karachi. In contemporary Pakistan, the public monument, now 'overwhelmingly militaristic in nature with sprinklings of calligraphic flourishes here and there', reflects changed 'national aspirations and aesthetic norms'. Simultaneously, 'calligraphic monuments have a longer shelf life and have consequently grown in number'. The 'interconnections, subliminal or otherwise, between these two kinds of monuments, the militaristic and calligraphic',[52] can be located within the ongoing search for a national modernist language that redresses the traumas of colonization and decolonization by aspiring, first, to an architectural internationalism and, subsequently, to a longing for vernacularism. While Indian modernism shows parallel impulses, what is striking in the case of Pakistan is calligraphy's return as a post-colonial public practice enacted in multiple registers – the monumental, as seen in Pakistan's 'roundabout art', the demotic, as manifested in the everyday visual profusion of Urdu script on the posters and billboards of Pakistan's streets, and, most significantly for this article, as remediations within contemporary visual art.[53]

READABLE, UNREADABLE, UNSPEAKABLE: CALLIGRAPHY AND PAKISTANI REGIONALISM

This reading of calligraphy in the Pakistani public sphere as a definite estrangement from calligraphy as script, and, therefore, as a symptom of trauma, is substantiated by its excessive visibility in the post-1971 years, peaking with General Zia-ul-Haq's Islamicization drive (1977–88).[54] The loss of Bangladesh being interpreted as a blow to the Two-Nation edifice, the state predictably responded by 'reworking its foundational myth to posit Jinnah and the Muslim League leadership as demanding Pakistan in order to establish not just a homeland for the nation of Indian Muslims, but an Islamic state'.[55] Calligraphy, South Asian Islamicate high culture's most visible signifier, was converted into a fetish, a substitute that marks an originary loss.[56] Art practice reflected this fetishizing impulse: 'thinking stultified and artists retreated behind the protection of formalism, one of its examples being arid calligraphy'.[57] But this stultification is only one aspect of calligraphy's place within Pakistani visual arts. From the 1950s onwards, artists working at an angle both to a pre-independence 'figurative tradition based on Indo-Muslim culture', exemplified in the work of Allah Bux and A.R. Chughtai,[58] and to the state's ideologies had constantly appropriated and re-worked this malleable signifier of Islamicate grandeur and post-colonial modernism,

Figure 2 *Teen Talwar* ('Three Swords') roundabout, Karachi. Photograph: Ananya Jahanara Kabir.

while reconfiguring their identity vis-à-vis the old and the new. As Akbar Naqvi asserts, 'most members of the art community felt the need to express their new, native identity'; yet 'very few', as Marcella Sirhandi reminds us, 'knew exactly what this was or how to express it visually'.[59] Calligraphy as cultural heritage was, for West Pakistani artists in the 1950s and the 1960s, an obvious source for a post-colonial identity, but their consequent remediation of script tended to fracture rather than confirm the nation's founding narratives.

If, for such artists, calligraphy became a metonym for an Islamic modernism that signified progress and internationalism as well as continuity with the Mughal past, remediating it also revealed that continuity as a *transplanted* one. Thus in the celebrated 'Roots' series by Anwar Jelal Shemza (1928–85), which depicts calligraphy in the form of trees with roots reaching below the soil, chromatics, surface texture and the very aspect of the calligraphic form together stand in complex dialogue with the Mughal inheritance. The image's unmistakable vernacularity abandons traditional styles to remediate script according to the visual trope of 'rootedness'. The morphing of remediation into pictorialism announces script's transplantation and re-rooting in different soil.[60] Exhibiting no longer the stately grace of Mughal calligraphy, but a new and arguably deliberate awkwardness, it now throbs with its own vivacity: this is the visual equivalent of Urdu spoken with the accents of the Punjab and Sind.[61] As Shemza exploits not only the 'visual properties of script but also its anxiety to be seen',[62] script exceeds its verbal significations to convey the post-colonial transformation of a heritage together with an optimism characteristic of pre-1971 Pakistan. This optimism suffuses, too, the 'action painting' of Ismail Gulgee (1926–2007), one of Pakistan's best-known modernist artists, which, in merging the motion of his body with Arabic calligraphy, 'was as close as Muslim art ever came to … the dance of the dervish'.[63] Yet such optimism was increasingly incompatible with 'the ambiguous relationship between Muslim nationalism and ethnic identities' that, already visible during the pre-independence years, was exacerbated by 'the authoritarianism of the modern state' that constrained 'the Pakistan state's capacity to resolve many of the conflicts arising from ethnicity'.[64] Script's contested history within colonial print capitalism, and the compromises with regional identities that its very aspect contained, haunted the calligraphed image.

Significantly, then, several of the early experimenters with script were of classic *muhajir* background. Their responses to the need to create a new visual identity out of the act of transplantation took divergent paths, as suggested by the contrast between Shakir Ali (1914–75), *muhajir* from Rampur, and Sadequain (1930–87), *muhajir* from Amroha (towns of the UP heartland).[65] Both were active during the 1960s in creating a visual register appropriate for the Pakistani state's modernist declarations. Shakir Ali's monumental calligraphic triptychs and murals adorned various state institutions, most tellingly the Atomic Energy Commission's headquarters in Islamabad, and, like 'the luscious curves of his Persian *nastaliq*', communicated an ostensible fidelity to Pakistan as the modern protector of Islamic tradition.[66] Dramatically different is Sadequain's 'calligraphic cubism' that made his 'commanding icon, the cactus as alif, the image of God as a calligraphic sign and his own emblem of self/ego'.[67] Metonymic of the deserts of Sindh, the 'cactus and its various metamorphosed images' became 'the most profound incorporation of Sindh into his art'.[68] In Sadequain's mural of 1965 commemorating the building of the Mangla Dam in Mirpur, 'large calligraphic or calligraphically derived outcrops loomed in [a] mythicized world of labour ... surrealistic, beyond explanation and even understanding'. But the seemingly meaningless juxtaposition of logically unrelated elements wrenches sense out of the subconscious terrain of loss and anxiety. The displacements induced by the developmental goals of the nation, figured in the Mangla Dam project that, ironically, motored most Mirpuri migration to the United Kingdom,[69] become silently connected with *muhajir* displacement. Remediation here becomes a comment not on re-rooting, but on the uprooting of populations that continues well beyond the happy ending of the Two-Nation story.

These difficulties in enunciating the conflicting demands of the state and the inner self were resolved through a progressive 'undecipherability [that] was the insistent condition of pure visibility'.[70] The calligraphic developments of Zahoor ul-Akhlaque (1941–2007) and Rasheed Ahmed Arshad (1937–) are instructive in this regard. In Zahoor's work during the 1960s, such as his 'Farman' ('edict') 1 and 2, both paintings whose subject matter is writing as edict, 'calligraphy as writing further regressed to linear marks' and 'clusters of vertical and horizontal long and short broken lines'.[71] Naqvi castigates Zahoor's calligraphic formalism as 'subversive without dividends', 'Brahminical', 'ritualistic' and 'arcane', contrasting it in particular with the similar undecipherability discernible in the calligraphic distortions of Arshad, but which he commends as successfully 'highlighting the functional and spiritual significance of writing, no less holy than prayer'.[72] Formally, the two artists certainly differ, with Arshad's calligraphy clearly referencing the traditional 'broken', shorthand script known as *shikasta*, also used for copying poetry and often metaphorically compared to the broken hearts lamented therein,[73] and Zahoor's performing a relentless reductionism of the calligraphic form. But their conceptual difference is perhaps more suggestive. Zahoor's work, which during the last two decades of his life was dominated by the trope of the torn page, declares, through unreadable faux-script, pessimism about the reconciliatory capacity of calligraphy as cultural inheritance. Arshad, however, revives through *shikasta* the talismanic quality of script. Courting esoteria as part of spiritual stocktaking, his remediated script reminds us that *shikasta*, 'reminiscent of modern graphics rather than legible script', is not so different from 'the most sacred, hieratic script' in the aesthetic and hermeneutic challenge it mounts to the would-be decipherer.[74]

Younger artists working out of Karachi are developing further such remediation of unreadable scripts. I began with Huma Mulji's *Mera ghar*, whose different scripts signify the sounds of Gujarati, Kutchi, Hindi, Sindhi and languages other than Urdu spoken in Karachi. Where shifts in accent can subsume this range of sounds into 'Urdu', the range of scripts currently unreadable to the average Pakistani rejects such subsumption by communicating the persistence of diversity and of identity confusion. The sculptor Jabbar Gul, of 'native' Sindhi rather than *muhajir* origin, conveys contemporary contestations around Pakistani identity through a very different version of unreadability. His wood sculptures incorporate an approximation of script on simulated *takhtis* or wooden slates. In 'Ten Commandments', a work comprising ten *takhtis* (of which one can be seen in Figure 3), the connection with writing is inescapable but ironic: 'Ten *takhtis* equal ten commandments. Everything is written but we don't follow them.' This visible feigning of script '[tries] to share something but [tries] to hide it as well: the script is between the lines'. Yet, this declaration of unreadable writtenness is different from Arshad's talismanic esoterism that recalls Islamic, and particularly Shia and Sufi, hermeneutics. It also breaks consciously with the calligraphic tradition. Agreeing that 'there is a connection between spirituality and my non-script', Gul nevertheless denies any 'connection with calligraphy and religion'.[75] Such contradictions are comprehensible through the visual impact of his faux-script. It looks nothing like Perso-Arabic; we are back with Shamsie's 'strange hieroglyphs'. Both from and based in Sindh, cradle of the Indus Valley civilization, and in, furthermore, an arts school named 'The Indus Valley School of Arts', Gul's ultimate signifier, I contend, is none other than the as-yet-undeciphered script of Mohenjodaro and Harappa.[76] This contention is explicable in the context of Pakistani Sindhi mobilization of the Indus civilization within separatist and regionalist assertions of identity.[77]

REMEDIATION AS REMEDY: FROM TRAUMA TOWARDS HEALING?

'What is written cannot be understood', comments Gul, 'or [perhaps] you don't want to understand it.'[78] In different yet broadly parallel ways, Mulji and Gul use script with all its layered associations to stake their equally different yet parallel claims to Karachi and to Sindh.[79] Such regionalism, anathema within the traditional context of Pakistani identity politics, is a trend increasingly visible in Pakistani cultural production. An inheritance of loss barely understood becomes necessary to figure out as the relationship of that inheritance with the assertions of subjectivities distanced from Partition by at least one generation. What is noteworthy is the range of unreadable scripts mobilized thereby, and their specific nuances. The Sanskrit-derived scripts that jostle against their Persian counterparts in *Mera ghar* announce an interest in cross-border regionalism that would unite Karachi, and Sind, with Gujarat, Kutch and Bombay in India – as aptly signalled by the creation of the poster for a cross-border art initiative. But Gul's allusions to the Indus Valley civilization speaks to a Sindhi revivalism that draws on the pre-Sanskrit, prehistorical layer of Mohenjodaro and Harappa to stake its nativist claims, as seen in the theory of 'Indus Man', proposed to great political effect by PPP leader Aitzaz Ahsan.[80] Attributing the creation of Pakistan to the culmination of a long-established cultural and historical Indus tradition which has moulded the Pakistani personality as distinct from the Indian, such theories attempt to establish a Pakistani identity rooted in the soil and history rather than in an 'obscurantist mould'.[81] This claim to the Indus is also being appropriated by non-Sindhis desiring to reconfigure post-1971 Pakistani identity within 'a shared common vision of the Indus region that constitutes present-day Pakistan'.[82]

Figure 3 Jabbar Gul, *Takhti* (wood cuts). Photograph: Ananya Jahanara Kabir.

Such appropriation and counter-appropriation signal a search for variously nested identities that can accommodate the range of displacements and affective legacies subtending the grand narratives of the nation's foundation.[83] At Lahore's 'Food Street' in September 2007, I sat at a stall whose signboard proclaimed items of Punjabi food in Gurmukhi and Shahmukhi, in order to be explicable, I was told, to Sikh pilgrims in Lahore (see Figure 4). This momentary disengagement of Punjabi from the script in which it is now written in West Punjab contrasts with its usual subsumption within a script identical to that used for Urdu, reaching out instead across the border in a manner not unlike the multiple scripts of Mulji's poster. Signboard and poster alike remind us how, in Pakistan, 'language and religion, rather than providing a panacea for unity in a plural society, have opened a Pandora's box of conflicting identities'.[84] Yet the lacuna Jalal observes for scholarship on Pakistan's genesis remains true for scholarship on contemporary Pakistan: 'The role of language as principal site of differential identity formation in north India and the Punjab has been more readily acknowledged than satisfactorily delineated.'[85] This article has attempted a modest advance by considering what script, remediated through Pakistani visual art, can tell us about that complex identity politics simultaneously stoked and elided by colonialism.[86] Covertly and overtly embodying forms of dissent to collectively sanctioned modes of self-fashioning, such remediation reveals script as a charged node for the intersection of discourses of religion, language and the pull of regionalism.

'The illegibility of calligraphy in the hands of its artists' has been suggestively interpreted as 'open[ing] up the phenomenon of textuality to index a constellation of identity in which elements from Africa, from Shiite vernacular culture or from Indo-Persian poetry all exceed the boundaries of nationality'.[87] Without denying the saliency of this reading, I would enfold its own orientation towards the cosmopolitan rather than the intra-national within an alternative understanding of remediated script as an acute, even distressed, representation of the dualities that Pakistan's cultural inheritance, as 'poetically Indo-Persian and discursively Arab', must straddle.[88] It is a particular irony that, though the visual aspect of script in Pakistan signals its westward gaze towards the 'classically' Islamicate cultures of Iran and the Middle East, and the corresponding rejection of an eastward orientation towards the vernacular worlds of South Asia, Pakistanis today can read the script of the former world without necessarily understanding the content of the form, while being able to comprehend what is being spoken and sung in the latter world, without being able to read what is written there.[89] This miasma of layered in/decipherabilities and in/comprehensions captures the cultural instability of contemporary Pakistan, where the elite cultural producer, literally caught between two stools, defaces his or her inherited script to the point of its determined illegibility without ever being able to erase from its cast the Islamicate sacrality that is its history and inheritance. Yet in these acts of defacement redemption can be glimpsed. The etymological relationship between 'remediate' and 'remedy' is an appropriate comment on how the remediation of script, in the artists I have examined, visualizes their fraught but necessary attempts towards healing Pakistani subjectivities of the multiple traumas through which all South Asian nations have come into modernity and into being, while conveying to us the specificity of that journey for Pakistan.[90]

Figure 4 Multiple scripts in Food Street, Lahore. Photograph: Ananya Jahanara Kabir.

ACKNOWLEDGEMENTS

This article draws on research conducted in Karachi and Lahore in September 2007. Thanks are due to: a British Academy Small Grant and Shisha (Manchester) for facilitating this visit; Naghma Butt of the Embassy of Pakistan, London; Ian Talbot and Neelam Srivastava for facilitating occasions where some of the propositions could be tested; Marta Bolognani, Nilofer Farrukh, Salima Hashmi, Aamer Hussein, Saira Kabir, Fareda Khan, Nukhbah Langah and Kamila Shamsie, who have, in different ways, helped me understand Pakistani cultural politics.

NOTES

1. Kamila Shamsie, *Kartography* (London: Bloomsbury, 2002); all quotes in this paragraph from pp. 340–1.
2. See *Aar-Paar 2002: Public Art Initiative between India and Pakistan*, http://members. tripod.com/aarpaar2/support.htm. For this project, Huma Mulji partnered with Mumbai-based artist Shilpa Gupta. Each created a poster and sent it to her counterpart, who then put it up in various public locations in her city. I am grateful to Huma Mulji for the conversation in Karachi, September 2007, for permission to reproduce the image, and for the words that I have used as my second epigraph.
3. See Ayesha Jalal, *Self and Sovereignty: Individual and Community in South Asian Islam since 1850* (Oxford and Delhi, 2000), pp. 102–33, for an excellent discussion about the complications between written script and oral language in the Punjab, the North West Provinces and the United Provinces that fed into the demand for Pakistan. For Karachi as a city of migrations and departures, see the novellas of Aamer Hussein, especially *Turquoise* (London, 2002), and the novels of Kamila Shamsie, especially *Kartography*.
4. Mulji's family is from Gujarat in western India, Shamsie's from present-day Uttar Pradesh in North India. The term *muhajir* theoretically means anyone who migrated from India to the new Pakistan, but it has a special resonance for the Urdu-speaking migrants who relocated to Karachi; see Ian Talbot, *India and Pakistan* (London, 2000), p. 199; Feroz Ahmed, *Ethnicity and Politics in Pakistan* (Karachi and Oxford, 1999); Vazira Fazila-Yacoobali Zamindar, *The Long Partition and the Making of Modern South Asia: Refugees, Boundaries, Histories* (New York, 2007).
5. 'The condition of "elseness", as distinct from what we have repeatedly been told about otherness, is one that is separate from the self and yet a part of it, certainly tied to it in a paradox of ambivalences' (Jalal, *Self and Sovereignty*, p. 571). This suggestive comment, made in the context of the relationship between Pakistani and Indian Muslims, is equally applicable to thinking about the relationship between Pakistani Muslims and the pre-Partition past of their families in what is now India.
6. See Zamindar, *The Long Partition*, p. 238; for instances of the early optimism, see Nafis Ahmad, with a foreword by H.S. Suhrawardy, *The Basis of Pakistan* (Calcutta, 1947); Mazhar Ali Khan, *Pakistan: The First Twelve Years: The Pakistan Times Editorials of Mazhar Ali Khan* (Karachi and Oxford, 1996).
7. By 'psychological dimension' I indicate the ways in which Partition has created a laminated and split subjectivity within people who have lived through Partition and those who have inherited it as 'postmemory', or the 'memory of a memory', where the latter pertains to a traumatic history; see Marianne Hirsch, *Family Frames: Photography, Narrative and Postmemory* (Cambridge, MA, 1997). For an examination of Partition's psychological

repercussions on the Indian Muslim, see Ananya Jahanara Kabir, 'Subjectivities, Memories, Loss: Of Pigskin Bags, Silver Spittoons, and the Partition of India', *Interventions*, 4(2) (2000), pp. 245–64.

8. For an overview, see the chapters devoted to Pakistan in Yashodhara Dalmia and Salima Hashmi (eds), *Memory, Metaphor, Mutations: Contemporary Art of India and Pakistan* (Delhi, 2007). For 'remediation', which is discussed in detail later in this article, see J. David Bolter and Richard Grusin, 'Remediation', *Configurations*, 4(3) (1996), pp. 311–58.

9. Iftikhar Dadi, 'Rethinking Calligraphic Modernism', in Kobena Mercer (ed.), *Discrepant Abstraction*, (Cambridge, MA, 2006), p. 105 (emphasis in the original); I engage further with Dadi's argument later in the article.

10. Thus even Dalmia and Hashmi's *Memory, Mutation, Metaphor* displays an imbalance between the six chapters devoted to India and the three devoted to Pakistan.

11. I refer to 'Partition: The Long Shadow', organized by the Heinrich Böll Foundation, Zubaan Books and the India Habitat Centre, Delhi (August 2007 to September 2008), see www.boell-india.org; 'Sohni Dharti' (August 2007), organized by Vasl and Shanaakht, Karachi, www.citizensarchive.org/schedule.shtml; and the conference 'The Independence of India and Pakistan: Sixtieth Anniversary Reflections' (July 2007), organized at the University of Southampton.

12. Recent, innovative scholarship includes: Zamindar, *The Long Partition*; Radha Kumar, *Making Peace with Partition* (New Delhi, 2005); Joya Chatterji, *The Spoils of Partition: Bengal and India, 1947–1967* (Cambridge, 2007); Suvir Kaul (ed.), *Partitions of Memory: The Afterlives of the Division of India* (New Delhi, 2001). Recent examples of Partition fiction in English include work by Kamila Shamsie from Pakistan, Siddhartha Deb writing on Partition and India's north-east, and Tehmima Anam from Bangladesh.

13. See Meenakshie Verma, *Aftermath: An Oral History of Violence* (New Delhi, 2004); Sukriti Paul Kumar, *Narrating Partition: Texts, Interpretations, Ideas* (New Delhi, 2004), and Gargi Chakravartty, *Coming out of Partition: Refugee Women of Bengal* (New Delhi and Calcutta, 2005), which do not advance the ground-breaking work represented by Urvashi Butalia, *The Other Side of Silence: Voices from the Partition of India* (New Delhi, 1999) and Ritu Menon and Kamla Bhasin, *Borders and Boundaries: Women in India's Partition* (New Delhi, 1998).

14. See the work of Ronald Bleiker, 'The Aesthetic Turn in International Political Theory', *Millennium: Journal of International Studies*, 30(3) (2001), pp. 551–28, 'Art after 9/11', *Alternatives*, 31 (2006), pp. 77–90, and 'Learning from Art: A Reply to Holden's Literature and World Politics', *Global Society*, 17(4) (2003), pp. 415–28.

15. Ananya Jahanara Kabir, 'Beyond Narrative: Song and Story in South Asia', *Moving Worlds: A Journal of Transcultural Writings*, 5(2) (2005), pp. 28–42.

16. See Elizabeth Deeds Ermarth, *Realism and Consensus: Time, Space and Narrative* (Edinburgh: Edinburgh University Press, 1998 [1983]); Martin Jay, 'Scopic Regimes of Modernity', in Hal Foster (ed.), *Vision and Visuality* (Seattle, WA, 1988), pp. 3–23; Martin Jay, *Downcast Eyes: The Denigration of Vision in Twentieth-Century French Thought* (Berkeley, CA, 1993), pp. 69–82; Bruno Latour, 'Drawing Things Together', in Michael Lynch and Steve Woolgar (eds), *Representation in Scientific Practice* (Cambridge, MA, 1990), pp. 19–68.

17. Krishna Kumar, *Prejudice and Pride: School Histories of the Freedom Struggle in India and Pakistan* (New Delhi, 2001).

18. See Simon Gikandi, *Maps of Englishness: Writing Identity in the Culture of Colonialism* (New York, 1996); Romila Thapar, *Narratives and the Making of History: Two Lectures* (New Delhi, 2000).

19. See Ananya Jahanara Kabir, *Territory of Desire: Representing the Valley of Kashmir* (Minneapolis, MN, 2009), especially chapter 5.

20. Ian Talbot, *Pakistan: A Modern History* (London: Hurst, 2005), pp. 4–6.

21. Kabir, 'Subjectivities, Memories, Loss'.

22. See Cathy Caruth (ed.), *Trauma: Explorations in Memory* (Baltimore and London, 1995) and *Unclaimed Experience: Trauma, Narrative and History* (Baltimore and London, 1996); Mieke Bal, Jonathan V. Crewe, and Leo Spitzer (eds), *Acts of Memory: Cultural Recall in the Present* (Hanover, NH, and London, 1999). On 'chosen trauma', see Vamik Volkan, *Bloodlines: From Ethnic Pride to Ethnic Terrorism* (Boulder, CO, 1998); for more on problematic consequences of narrative for conflict, see Lisa Malkki, *Purity and Exile: Violence, Memory and National Cosmology among Hutu Refugees in Tanzania* (Chicago, IL: University of Chicago Press, 1999) and Mahmood Mamdani, *When Victims Become Killers: Colonialism, Nativism, and the Genocide in Rwanda* (Oxford, 2001).

23. Akbar Naqvi, *Image and Identity: Fifty Years of Painting and Sculpture in Pakistan* (Oxford and Delhi, 1998), p. xxxi.

24. For a useful overview, see Marcella Nissom Sirhandi, *Contemporary Painting in Pakistan* (Lahore, 1992) and Salima Hashmi et al. (eds), *Moving Ahead* (Islamabad, 2007), the catalogue of the opening exhibition of the National Art Gallery, Islamabad.

25. On 'hypermediacy', see Svetlana Alpers, *The Art of Describing: Dutch Art in the Seventeenth Century* (Chicago, IL, 1983).

26. On the 'hybrid' 'Imagetext', see W.J.T. Mitchell, *Picture Theory* (Chicago, IL, 1994).

27. Bolter and Grusin, 'Remediation'.

28. Bolter and Grusin, 'Remediation', p. 339.

29. James A.W. Heffernan, 'Ekphrasis and Representation', *New Literary History*, 22(2) (Spring 1991), pp. 299, 300.

30. Heffernan, 'Ekphrasis', p. 301. On rivalry in remediation, see Bolter and Grusin, 'Remediation', p. 339.

31. W.J.T. Mitchell, *Iconology: Image, Text, Ideology* (Chicago, IL, 1986), p. 43; also quoted in Neil Ten Kortenaar, 'Postcolonial Ekphrasis: Salman Rushdie Gives the Finger Back to the Empire', *Contemporary Literature*, 38(2) (Summer 1997), pp. 232–59.

32. Ten Kortenaar, 'Postcolonial Ekphrasis', p. 242.

33. Sorayya Khan, *Noor* (Harmondsworth, 2003).

34. Annemarie Schimmel, *Calligraphy and Islamic Culture* (London, 1990), p. 1.

35. Schimmel, *Calligraphy*, p. 25.

36. Franz Rosenthal, 'Significant Uses of Arabic Writing', in *Four Essays on Art and Literature in Islam* (Leiden, 1971), p. 59.

37. Jalal, *Self and Sovereignty*, p. 47.

38. Robert Fraser, *Book History through Postcolonial Eyes: Rewriting the Script* (London, 2008), p. 114; see pp. 111–14 for a thorough discussion of the technology of lithography and its development in India and Persia as an alternative to metal-forged typeface.

39. David Lelyveld, 'The Fate of Hindustani', in Carol Breckenridge and Peter Van der Veer (eds), *Orientalism and the Postcolonial Predicament* (Philadelphia, PA, 1993), p. 202; see also Francesca Orsini, *The Hindi Public Sphere 1920–1940: Language and Literature in the Age of Nationalism* (New York, 2002), p. 21.

40. Paul Brass, *Language, Religion and Politics in North India* (Cambridge, 1974), quoted in Orsini, *Hindi Public Sphere*, p. 23.

41. Jalal, *Self and Sovereignty*, p. 100.

42. Hashmi, *Moving Ahead*, p. 47.

43. See Orsini, *Hindi Public Sphere*, chapter 1; on orality, see further Michael Nijhawan,

'Partition Violence in Memory and Performance: The Punjabi Dhadi Tradition', in Smitha Tewari Jassal and Eyal Ben-Ari (eds), *The Partition Motif in Contemporary Conflicts* (New Delhi, 2007), pp. 145–65.

44. Jalal, *Self and Sovereignty*, p. 104.
45. Jalal, *Self and Sovereignty*, p. 135.
46. Jalal, *Self and Sovereignty*, p. 135.
47. Talbot, *Pakistan*, p. 27.
48. Jalal, *Self and Sovereignty*, p. 112.
49. Philip Oldenburg, '"A Place Insufficiently Imagined": Language, Belief, and the Pakistan Crisis of 1971', *Journal of Asian Studies*, 44(4) (1985), pp. 711–33; Talbot, *Pakistan*, p. 90.
50. Schimmel, *Calligraphy*, p. 33.
51. See Wijdan Ali, *Modern Islamic Art: Development and Continuity* (Gainesville, FL, 1997), chapters 15 and 16. Dadi, in 'Rethinking Calligraphic Modernism', places the Pakistani artist Sadequain's work between 1955 and 1975 amongst artists from Sudan, Iran and Iraq in order to offer comparative comments on calligraphic modernism during the high noon of decolonization; similar observations for Indonesia are made by Kenneth M. George, 'Picturing Aceh: Violence, Religion and a Painter's Tale', in Andrew C. Wilford and Kenneth M. George (eds), *Spirited Politics: Religion and Politics in Contemporary South Asia* (Ithaca, NY, 2005), pp. 195–208, and for Iran by Judith Ernst, 'The Problem of Islamic Art', in Miriam Cooke and Bruce M. Lawrence (eds), *Muslim Networks from Hajj to Hiphop* (Chapel Hill, NC, 2005), pp. 107–32.
52. This and the three preceding quotations are from Salima Hashmi, 'The Intensity of Space and Substance', in *Moving Ahead*, p. 62. See also Talbot, *India and Pakistan*, p. 215.
53. On Pakistani architecture and modernism, see Quddus Mirza, 'Fusion and Profusion', *ArtIndia*, 12(4) (2007), pp. 67–9, and also for Karachi's distinctive modernism, ibid., p. 69.
54. On the Zia regime, see Talbot, *India and Pakistan*, pp. 201, 209–11; see also Iftikhar Dadi, 'Political Posters in Karachi, 1988–1999', *South Asian Popular Culture*, 5(1) (2007), pp. 11–30.
55. Talbot, *Pakistan*, p. 5.
56. This fetishizing of calligraphy is also a feature of pan-Islamic modernity, as the work of Iranian artist Shirin Neshat complexly gestures towards; see Iftikhar Dadi, 'Shirin Neshat's Photographs as Postcolonial Allegories', *Signs: Journal of Women in Culture and Society*, 34(1) (2008), pp. 125–50. For a theoretical argument for the connections between nationalism, trauma and fetishism, see Kabir, *Territory of Desire*.
57. Naqvi, *Image and Identity*, p. xxxiv.
58. Sirhandi, *Contemporary Painting*, p. 22.
59. Naqvi, *Image and Identity*, p. 1; Sirhandi, *Contemporary Painting*, p. 20.
60. On 'pictorialism', see Heffernan, 'Ekphrasis', pp. 299–300.
61. Shemza's career and post-1947 life took him both to Lahore and to Karachi before he finally emigrated to London. See Sirhandi, *Contemporary Painting*, pp. 47–8.
62. Naqvi, *Image and Identity*, p. 282.
63. Naqvi, *Image and Identity*, pp. 360–1; Sirhandi, *Contemporary Painting*, pp. 59–60.
64. Talbot, *Pakistan*, p. 6.
65. Naqvi, *Image and Identity*, p. 253; Sirhandi, *Contemporary Painting*, pp. 60–1.
66. Naqvi, *Image and Identity*, pp. 251, 253.
67. Naqvi, *Image and Identity*, pp. 401–3.
68. Naqvi, *Image and Identity*, pp. 394–5.
69. Patricia Ellis and Zafar Khan, 'Kashmiri Displacement and the Impact on Kashmiriyat', *Contemporary South Asia*, 12 (2003), pp. 523–38.

70. Naqvi, *Image and Identity*, pp. 282–3.
71. Naqvi, *Image and Identity*, pp. 455, 458.
72. Naqvi, *Image and Identity*, pp. 458, 460, 464.
73. Schimmel, *Calligraphy*, p. 31.
74. See Schimmel, *Calligraphy*, p. 31.
75. Jabbar Gul, in conversation with the author, Karachi, September 2007.
76. See Nayanjot Lahiri (ed.), *The Decline and Fall of the Indus Civilization* (Delhi, 2000) and *Forgotten Cities: How the Indus Civilization Was Discovered* (Delhi, 2006).
77. I am grateful to Javed Majeed for alerting me to this point.
78. Jabbar Gul, in conversation with the author, Karachi, September 2007.
79. For which see S.D. Ansari, *Life after Partition: Migration, Community and Strife in Sindh, 1947–1962* (New York, 2005).
80. Aitzaz Ahsan, *The Indus Saga and the Making of Pakistan* (Karachi and Oxford, 1996).
81. Talbot, *Pakistan*, p. 18.
82. Hashmi, *Moving Ahead*, p. 13.
83. Katherine Adeney, *Federalism and Ethnic Conflict Regulation in India and Pakistan* (New York, 2007); Ahmed, *Ethnicity and Politics*.
84. Talbot, *Pakistan*, p. 1.
85. Jalal, *Self and Sovereignty*, p. 102.
86. Jalal, *Self and Sovereignty*, p. 101.
87. Dadi, 'Rethinking Calligraphic Modernism', p. 105.
88. Ibid.
89. I am grateful to Girish Shahane for this observation. This tendency of the westward gaze is apparent even in Dadi's otherwise superb analysis of calligraphic modernism within Pakistani art in 'Rethinking Calligraphic Modernism', which looks resolutely towards Iran, Iraq and Sudan without considering the Indic complications to the Pakistani heritage at and beyond the moment of decolonization.
90. Both derive from Latin *remederi* ('to heal', 'to restore to health'); see Bolter and Grusin, 'Remediation', p. 350.

REVIEW ESSAY

INTERDISCIPLINARITY AND THE HISTORY OF EMOTIONS

Willemijn Ruberg

Department of History and Art History, Utrecht University

Keywords: emotions, interdisciplinarity, historiography, gender

In recent years, a vast number of books, emanating from disciplines such as psychology, neuroscience, history and literary theory, have discussed the phenomenon of emotion. Philosophers have been analysing emotions, or rather passions or sentiments, for centuries and, since the arrival of psychology as a discipline, the study of affect has been part of that burgeoning field.[1] Emotions have been studied by historians as well, from the middle of the nineteenth century. The Dutch historian Johan Huizinga used emotion to characterize the spirit of the late Middle Ages; the French *Annales* scholar Lucien Febvre took seriously the analysis of emotions as objects of historical enquiry; and German sociologist Norbert Elias's work on the civilizing process revolved around emotion and self-control.[2] However, only with the rise of social and cultural history since the 1970s and 1980s have emotions increasingly been paid serious attention.[3] I cannot do justice here to the many interesting works that have appeared since then, but will comment on those historians who have most advanced methodological and theoretical debates in the study of emotion.

In her overview of the historiography on emotion (published 2002), Barbara Rosenwein criticizes the simplistic narrative of emotional development through history associated with Elias's *The Civilizing Process*, in which the Middle Ages are depicted as a period during which people childishly expressed all emotions without restraint and the early modern period is seen as a time of increasing emotional control, culminating in the self-discipline of the modern period.[4] Rosenwein terms this the 'hydraulic model' (referring to emotions as liquids within each person eager to be let out).[5] Two of the historians Rosenwein takes issue with are Carol Zisowitz Stearns and Peter Stearns, who have nonetheless made a major contribution to the study of emotions. In their study of anger in the USA in the nineteenth and twentieth centuries, they coined a new concept – 'emotionology' – defined as the 'collective emotional standards of a society'.[6] For the Stearnses, emotionology belongs to the modern period, when advice

Address for correspondence: Willemijn Ruberg, Department of History and Art History, Utrecht University, Drift 10, 3512 BS Utrecht, The Netherlands. E-mail: W.G.Ruberg@uu.nl

Cultural and Social History, Volume 6, Issue 4, pp. 507–516 © The Social History Society 2009
DOI 10.2752/147800409X467631

manuals for the middle classes originated. According to Rosenwein, this view prohibits serious study of emotional standards in earlier times, including her own early medieval field, and avoids the important question of how individuals internalize or resist those standards.[7]

In her article, Rosenwein identified several problems within the historiography of emotion: the role of emotions in the coming of modernity, the association of emotions with irrationality, and the relationship between communal emotional standards and individual feelings. She pointed out two major theoretical responses to the 'hydraulic model'. Firstly, from the 1960s cognitive psychologists traced the origins of emotion to the mind rather than the body. They viewed emotions as resulting from rational individual judgements about the harmfulness or advantage of a situation. Secondly, in the 1970s social constructionists regarded both the emotion and its expression as shaped by society.[8] Later, post-structuralists would claim that an emotion expressed in language has no referent to a 'real', felt, emotion. For historians, this poses the important question: can we recover or represent (individual/collective) emotions of the past?

Writing in 2005, Peter Burke identified four main problems encountered by historians of emotion: the problem of defining emotions; the problem of relating emotions to particular social groups; the problem of 'concepts, methods and theories'; and the problem of sources.[9] In this review article I will show that these problems still preoccupy historians, especially the questions of definition and theory. Specifically, I will address the issue of interdisciplinarity in research on emotions, which raises urgent questions given the pace of research into emotions in neuroscience and psychology. Should historians incorporate the latest findings of research in the natural and social sciences or does literary and cultural theory provide us with better models? Conversely, should natural and social scientists also pay more attention to the views of cultural historians? I will try to answer these questions by focusing on the following three recently published books: rhetoric scholar Daniel M. Gross's *The Secret History of Emotion: From Aristotle's Rhetoric to Modern Brain Science* (2006); (developmental) psychologist Jerome Kagan's *What Is Emotion? History, Measures, and Meanings* (2007); and historian Martha Tomhave Blauvelt's *The Work of the Heart: Young Women and Emotion 1780–1830* (2007).[10] In addition, I will incorporate an analysis of some of the papers presented at five panels on the history of emotion at the European Social Science History Conference (ESSHC) in Lisbon, which was held from 26 February to 1 March 2008.

Cultural historian William M. Reddy has so far published the most interdisciplinary work within the history of emotions, paying serious attention to psychological and anthropological research into emotion. Reddy's work, culminating in his monograph *The Navigation of Feeling: A Framework for the History of Emotions* (2001), is remarkable in several respects. Firstly, he based his proposals on the latest research in psychology which suggested that emotions are cognitive habits that can be learned and unlearned in interaction with the surrounding culture, rather than biologically pre-programmed responses. When it comes to the body–mind dichotomy, Reddy can thus be regarded as a cognitive theorist. Secondly, Reddy signalled an impasse in recent anthropological research into the emotions. Referring to linguist J.L. Austin's distinction between constatives (statements that describe reality) and performatives (statements that construct a situation, like 'I thee wed'), he drew a parallel with statements about emotions. These can be regarded as descriptive (the utterance accurately referring to a felt emotion) or performative (social constructionists think a statement about an emotion immediately *creates* that particular emotion). In anthropology, the first view was seen as too simplistic, but Reddy also expressed concern about the anti-essentialism of social constructionist anthropological work, which he viewed as tantamount to anti-humanism. Reddy did not agree with the social constructionist view of emotional utterances as being purely self-referential (not referring to an internally felt emotion). He regarded statements about emotions as performative in the sense that they do change things, but not as (only) self-referential: rather, they change the state of the speaker or of the surrounding environment.[11] Instead, Reddy coined the term 'emotives': 'Emotives are influenced directly by, and alter, what they "refer" to [....] Emotives do things to the world.'[12]

By inventing the term 'emotive', Reddy hoped to find a way out of the relativism offered by social constructionists, who in his opinion made a meaningful history of emotions impossible by their exclusive focus on emotional discourse, neglecting individual agency and avoiding any statement of the universality of emotions. Testing his theory of emotions and historical change on Revolutionary France, particularly on the demise of sentimentalism under the Terror, Reddy distanced himself from post-structuralism. Reddy can thus be regarded as part of the 'performative turn' by emphasizing the (open-ended) effects of emotions performed by individual agents.[13]

Reddy's work has been influential within the historiography of emotion, although it has received some critique.[14] One could question, for example, his reductive summary of post-structuralist positions on emotion. Literary theorist Rei Terada, who does not refer to the work of Reddy, proposes a more complex view of a number of post-structuralist theorists.[15] She states that critics have accused deconstructionists like Derrida of reducing all experiences, including emotions, to textual traces, thereby only allowing for the study of representations of emotions rather than emotions themselves. Terada, however, emphasizes that we cannot pin down the definition of an emotion; rather, it is the openness of the representation that evokes an affect:

> It is not possible to talk about what emotion is, however, apart from arguments about how it can be conceived. It is only possible to construct a theory of emotion – or of anything – by asking how to represent it. The difficulty of representing emotion, in other words, *is* the difficulty of knowing what it is, not just for poststructuralist theory but for any theory.[16]

Terada defies the secondary literature that assumes that post-structuralists do not have an account of emotion; she aims to show how emotional effects are pervasive in post-structuralist theory, particularly in the work of Derrida, de Man and Deleuze, and how these are non-subjective (Derrida, for instance, locating emotions in relations rather than subjects).[17] Importantly, Terada expands and combines classical models of subjectivity – such as that of Descartes, in which emotions are a vital part of the thinking being – with models that disconnect subjectivity from emotion, such as Freudian or Foucauldian approaches.[18] This point would imply for historians that they should be open to the presence of emotions apart from those explicit emotional utterances by subjects, for example by looking at structures that facilitate, entail or hide emotions.

In short, even though from opposing standpoints, both Terada and Reddy show the political significance of theory on emotion: emotions are connected with subjectivity, agency and therefore humanity. The political implications of the study of emotions become particularly clear in Daniel M. Gross's book *The Secret History of Emotion*. Studying texts ranging from Aristotle to early modern sermons and from sentimental novels to modern neuroscience, Gross traces the transformation of the Aristotelian, rhetorical tradition that regarded emotions as social and political into the 'generalized psychology' (starting in the Age of Sensibility) which assumed that we all share the same hardwired emotions.[19] He argues against the idea common in biology and neuroscience that we all have similar brains and thus similar emotions. Gross instead takes Aristotle and the early modern appropriation of his work as a starting point, focusing on the idea that emotions are thoroughly social:

> The contours of our emotional world have been shaped by institutions such as slavery and poverty that simply afford some people greater emotional range than others, as they are shaped by publicity that has nothing to do with the inherent value of each human life and everything to do with technologies of social recognition and blindness.[20]

The social side of emotions forms a secret history, written out of mainstream history that, according to Gross, only pays attention to emotions as biological phenomena. Although Gross's text is certainly well written and throws new light on the use of rhetoric by studying diverse sources, he does not sufficiently take into account previous (historical and sociological) studies of emotions that have equally emphasized the social aspect of emotions.[21] In addition, one might ask whether his interpretation of a scholar like Antonio Damasio is not too one-sided.[22] Gross takes issue with neuroscientist Damasio, who regards emotions mostly as embodied and neurophysiological phenomena. In *Descartes' Error: Emotion, Reason and the Human Brain* (1994), Damasio claimed that the Cartesian separation between body and mind, with its accompanying valuation of the rational mind, neglects the important connections between body, brain and emotions, shown by neuroscientific research. Rather, emotions are conducive to reason, social and ethical behaviour.[23] Gross regards this view as too simplistic and 'biological': neuroscientists like Damasio are, according to Gross, 'not studying the social brain with an adequate understanding of what it means to be social, and they are certainly not improving society, as Damasio ultimately wishes to do'.[24]

However, other historians, like Hera Cook, prefer to take from Damasio a much more complex view on emotions. Cook follows Damasio in claiming that emotions have a bodily component, thereby arguing against cognitive theorists like Martha Nussbaum and William Reddy, who define emotions as forms of intelligent awareness which supply the organism with essential aspects of practical reason.[25] By defining emotions as cognitive, thereby neglecting the body and assuming that it cannot be socially constructed (a view that has been strongly criticized in recent years),[26] these theorists emphasize instead the socially constructed aspect of the emotions. According to this view, only those feelings aimed at an object are 'emotions', thereby excluding 'purely' physical sensations. Cook, however, maintains that to recognize that emotions have a bodily component does not mean they cannot be regarded as socially constructed. In Damasio's view, the mind is composed of interactions between body and brain and a separation between the two, the Cartesian dualism, would therefore be artificial. Hence, Cook, in her research into sexuality and emotional control in twentieth-century England, pays attention to embodied emotions without losing sight of cultural and social norms.[27]

In short, Gross and Cook read Damasio differently. Gross is more specifically concerned with the political implications of Damasio's scientific work, as well as with the psycho-physiological notion that emotions are equally distributed. Like Terada, Gross is sensitive to the automatic association of emotion with a certain definition of subjectivity. He warns, for instance, against projecting a 'postmodern' active/passive divide onto the early modern period, whereby activity is associated with subjectivity, and he shows how in Civil War England the emotion of 'humility', or passivism toward the self, was directly related with activism towards the community.[28] Thus, Gross shows how the relationship between emotions and subjectivity is historically variable. The value of his book lies particularly in his emphasis on the political implications of studying emotion, a perspective that should be kept in mind by scientists, who, on the contrary, often claim they are motivated by the scientific quest to find the ultimate seat and cause of emotions.

Psychologist Jerome Kagan, in his book *What Is Emotion?* (aimed at a broad readership), maintains that emotions have received the attention of many scholars because they serve many functions, such as alarming a person to pain, aiding memory or motivating sexual reproduction.[29] Kagan provides an overview of scientific studies into emotion, warning against premature celebration of having found the answer to the puzzle of emotion, and he makes several key points. Firstly, he sees emotions as psychological phenomena. Although he contends that every emotion originates in brain activity, each brain profile can lead to an envelope of emotions and the specific emotion that emerges depends on the context, the person's history and biology. Kagan here argues against the sole reliance on brain states by neuroscientists like Damasio, who are not interested in conscious feelings or their evaluations as definitions of emotions. He also argues against behaviourists, who want to predict a certain feeling from a particular brain state on the assumption that rewards strengthen habits. Kagan insists that not every change in brain state in response to an incentive necessarily leads to the production of a feeling. Secondly, Kagan identifies as problematic the desire to divide the potentially large number of emotional states into a small, tidy category of fundamental emotions and a large, messy set of less basic states; there is a clear lack of consensus over such a division. In connection with this, Kagan pays serious attention to the (cultural and historical) variance of words used to describe affect. He rightly asks: 'Should feelings be classified in accord with their consequences, origins, brain profiles, or semantic descriptions?'[30]

Kagan is of the opinion that a brain state that fails to produce a conscious feeling or action should not be regarded as an emotion and questions limiting the term 'emotion' to states that have functional consequences. He is also sceptical of the claim that a small number of basic emotions can be identified.[31] Moreover, he is critical of transposing the findings of research on animals to human beings and unravels all kinds of cultural presuppositions in research by scientists who claim to be neutral. On the one hand, therefore, Kagan is very much aware that defining an emotion is a cultural construction, and he does refer to historical examples by briefly mentioning Thomas Aquinas, Freud and Darwin to show how the ethics, consciousness and consequences of feelings took centre stage before neuroscience and sociobiology focused on sensory pleasures and biological fitness. He also shows sensitivity to the intricate nature–nurture debate when it comes to gender and class differences in emotions, taking into account hormones and biological predispositions but ultimately stressing culture's overriding influence. So while Kagan might be classified as a social constructionist, when making historical comparisons it transpires he is not very familiar with historical studies on emotion, which occasionally leads to anachronistic reasoning and speculation, such as: 'I suspect that sexual feelings possessed greater salience during the nineteenth century than they do today because there was greater response uncertainty over their expression.'[32]

Thus, although Kagan's perception of emotions as culturally and historically constructed has to be appreciated, overall his historical comparison (admittedly only a minor part of his book) is weak. However, his main points regarding the definition of emotions show how some psychologists have incorporated a social constructionist perspective. The question remains as to whether historians should follow the latest research in neuroscience and psychology when it comes to looking for a definition of emotion. Martha Tomhave Blauvelt is probably wise in abstaining from choosing one definition of emotion in her book *The Work of the Heart: Young Women and Emotion 1780–1830*. This does not mean, however, that, in analysing the emotional world of American women in the early republic, she does not borrow concepts from the social sciences; rather, the work of sociologists Erving Goffman and Arlie Hochschild are carefully deployed. Indeed, Hochschild's concept of 'emotion work', stressing the efforts people make to perform emotions, accompanied by rewards and costs, turns out to be very appropriate in the study of late eighteenth and early nineteenth century American women's diaries. Hochschild considers emotion to be a process rather than a thing and Tomhave Blauvelt shows how young women dealt with the emotional demands of their surrounding culture, including the cult of sensibility. She shows how different women 'performed' emotions in response to these rules and therefore how diaries functioned as 'emotives' (Reddy) or tools of emotion management.[33] Tomhave Blauvelt has organized her book around Rosenwein's concept of 'emotional communities', indicating how women travelled between different emotional communities including the family, boarding school and the village, as well as imagined emotional communities, such as those of readers affiliated through print media.

Although it is a pity the emotional culture of men is not studied, which would have provided an interesting comparison to women's diaries and an antidote to the association of emotion with women, *The Work of the Heart* is a book that brings individuals' emotions to life. The fourth chapter, entitled 'Losing it: Anger and the Boundaries of Female Behaviour', is the most interesting. Here Tomhave Blauvelt significantly readjusts historians' ideas on the extent to which women could express anger. Whereas Peter and Carol Zisowitz Stearns located a new cultural deterrence against expressing anger in the eighteenth century for both men and women, historians of the later nineteenth century have argued that the expression of anger was strictly forbidden for women. Tomhave Blauvelt, however, found that many American women did ventilate their anger in their diaries. Although this ventilation was discouraged by the cult of sensibility and rarely expressed in public, especially women with a strong sense of self did write about outrage, mostly precipitated by 'issues of identity for both themselves and others, and in that sense, fear of losing the self'; this included anxiety over male deceit and preoccupation with their reputations in courtship.[34] Tomhave Blauvelt shows how diverse women in the early republic used their emotional culture to construct the self, indicating important generational differences. Young, single women experienced a strong sense of self and agency, which often disappeared after marriage, caused not only by a busy family life but also by the strong decrease in reading that had previously provided the language for emotional self-expression. Through the concept of 'emotion work', Tomhave Blauvelt also wants to provide a new way of conceptualizing the gendered separation of the public and private spheres, as well as the distinction between self and community, binaries that she, in common with other historians, does not find useful.[35] She sees the lines between individual and communal selves, as well as those between public and private, as fluid: 'the self was a fluid entity negotiated as emotion was constructed'.[36] Again, the importance of emotions to subjectivity comes to the fore.

To conclude, the relevance of the study of emotions to subjectivity and human agency is particularly felt in the disciplines of history and literary theory. Psychology and neuroscience seem much more preoccupied with attaining a perfect definition of emotion. Nevertheless, historians also still struggle with this question of definition, since definitions seem to pin down the historically variable phenomenon of emotions. Reddy coined a new phrase, 'emotives', to circumvent regarding emotional statements as simple descriptions of bodily feelings, on the one hand, or self-referential discourses on the other. Reddy thereby tried explicitly to address post-structuralist relativism, which in his view obstructs the study of historical change. At the same time, he emphasized the performative aspects of emotions: what do they *do*? This question paves the way for a more ethical and political perspective, hinted at by, for example, Gross, who also criticizes scientists for referring to human universals without taking into account social differences and inequalities. Yet, it is questionable whether psychologists and neuroscientists completely neglect the latter. Although some work from those disciplines still seems to take place in a political and social vacuum,[37] Kagan shows that psychologists are increasingly preoccupied with the cultural construction of emotions and its social implications. As the neuroscientist Steven Rose argues: 'Nothing makes sense in biology except in the context of history – and within history I include evolution, development, social, cultural and technological history.'[38] If Anna Green is correct in predicting the rediscovery of the individual in cultural history, to which a study of emotions is of central importance, then historians and natural scientists will have to take more notice of each other's research.[39]

ACKNOWLEDGEMENTS

I would like to thank Kristine Steenbergh, Karen Schaller, Katherine O'Donnell, Sinéad McDermott and the two anonymous reviewers for their helpful comments on previous versions of this article.

NOTES

1. Often the word 'emotion' is distinguished from 'affect', the latter referring mostly to a primary, non-conscious, bodily experience, whereas the former would indicate a more psychological, interpretive experience. I use the two words interchangeably in this article. Also see Thomas Dixon, *From Passions to Emotions: The Creation of a Secular Psychological Category* (Cambridge, 2003); Fay Bound Alberti (ed.), *Medicine, Emotion and Disease, 1700–1950* (Basingstoke, 2006).
2. Johan Huizinga, *The Autumn of the Middle Ages* [1919], trans. Rodney J. Payton and Ulrich Mammitzsch (Chicago, 1996); Lucien Febvre, 'Sensibility and History' [1941], in Peter Burke (ed.), *A New Kind of History: From the Writings of Febvre*, trans. Keith Folca (New York, 1973), pp. 27–43; Norbert Elias, *The Civilizing Process* [1939], trans. Edmund Jephcott, 2 vols (Oxford, 1981–2).
3. For an overview, see Peter Burke, 'Is There a Cultural History of the Emotions?', in Penelope Gouk and Helen Hills (eds), *Representing Emotions: New Connections in the Histories of Art, Music and Medicine* (Aldershot, 2005), pp. 35–47.
4. Barbara H. Rosenwein, 'Worrying about Emotions in History', *American Historical Review*, 107 (2002), pp. 821–7.
5. Rosenwein, 'Worrying about Emotions in History', p. 834.
6. Peter N. Stearns and Carol Z. Stearns, 'Emotionology: Clarifying the History of Emotions and Emotional Standards', *American Historical Review*, 90 (1985), pp. 813–36. Carol Zisowitz Stearns and Peter N. Stearns, *Anger: The Struggle for Emotional Control in America's History* (Chicago, 1986); Peter N. Stearns, *Jealousy: The Evolution of an Emotion in American History* (New York, 1989).
7. Rosenwein, 'Worrying about Emotions in History', p. 842. For the question of internalization, see Michael Roper, 'Slipping out of View: Subjectivity and Emotion in Gender History', *History Workshop Journal*, 59 (2005), pp. 57–72, and Joanna Bourke, 'Fear and Anxiety: Writing about Emotion in Modern History', *History Workshop Journal*, 55 (2003), pp. 111–33.
8. Rosenwein, 'Worrying about Emotions in History', p. 837.
9. Burke, 'Is There a Cultural History of the Emotions?', pp. 38–9. Also see the special issue of *Textual Practice* based on a selection of papers given at a 2004 colloquium 'Languages of Emotion', and especially the introduction: Emma Mason and Isobel Armstrong, 'Introduction: "Feeling: An Indefinite Dull Region of the Spirit?"', *Textual Practice*, 22 (2008), pp. 1–19. Also see Adela Pinch, 'Emotion and History: A Review Article', *Comparative Studies in Society and History*, 37 (1995), pp. 100–9.
10. Daniel M. Gross, *The Secret History of Emotion: From Aristotle's Rhetoric to Modern Brain Science* (Chicago and London, 2006); Jerome Kagan, *What Is Emotion? History, Measures,*

and *Meanings* (New Haven, CT, and London, 2007); Martha Tomhave Blauvelt, *The Work of the Heart: Young Women and Emotion 1780–1830* (Charlottesville, VA, and London, 2007).

11. William M. Reddy, 'Against Constructionism: The Historical Ethnography of Emotions', *Current Anthropology*, 38 (1997), p. 331.

12. William M. Reddy, *The Navigation of Feeling: A Framework for the History of Emotions* (Cambridge, 2001), p. 105.

13. Reddy himself refused to use the term 'performative', since he wanted to avoid the post-structuralist, self-referential connotation, as he saw it, in, for example, Judith Butler's work; Reddy, 'Against Constructionism', p. 328, footnote 2. The performative nature of emotions is mostly studied by queer theorists: see, for example, Eve Kosofsky Sedgwick, *Touching Feeling: Affect, Pedagogy, Performativity* (Durham, NC, 2003). Also see William M. Reddy, 'The Logic of Action: Indeterminacy, Emotion, and Historical Narrative', *History and Theory*, 40 (2001), pp. 10–33.

14. For an extensive review of Reddy's book, see James Smith Allen, 'Navigating the Social Sciences: A Theory for the Meta-history of Emotions', *History and Theory*, 42 (2003), pp. 82–93.

15. Rei Terada, *Feeling in Theory: Emotion after the 'Death of the Subject'* (Cambridge and London, 2001).

16. Ibid., 41. Also see Karen Schaller, 'Secrecy and Textual Affect: The Case for Re-reading Emotion in Elizabeth Bowen's "Tears, Idle Tears"', Paper for the ESSHC, 2008, http://www2.iisg.nl/esshc/programme.asp?selyear=9&pap=7004 (accessed 22 September 2008).

17. Terada, *Feeling in Theory*, p. 45.

18. Ibid., pp. 9–10.

19. Gross, *Secret History of Emotion*, p. 8.

20. Ibid., p. 4.

21. Gross mentions neither Reddy's *The Navigation of Feeling* nor, for instance, Sara Ahmed's *The Cultural Politics of Emotion* (New York, 2004), nor the historical work on emotion by Peter and Carol Stearns. He only refers to sociologist Arlie Russell Hochschild's important work on emotion *The Managed Heart: Commercialization of Human Feeling* (Berkeley, CA, 2003) in a footnote on p. 177.

22. Also see Michael J. Hyde, 'Book Review of *The Secret History of Emotion: From Aristotle's "Rhetoric" to Modern Brain Science*', *Philosophy and Rhetoric*, 40 (2007), p. 328.

23. Antonio Damasio, *Descartes' Error: Emotion, Reason, and the Human Brain* (New York, 2000). Gross also critiques Antonio Damasio, *The Feeling of What Happens: Body and Emotion in the Making of Consciousness* (New York, 1999) and Antonio Damasio, *Looking for Spinoza: Joy, Sorrow, and the Feeling Brain* (New York, 2003).

24. Gross, *Secret History of Emotion*, p. 35.

25. See Martha C. Nussbaum, *Upheavals of Thought: The Intelligence of Emotions* (Cambridge, 2001).

26. See Zoltán Kövecses, *Metaphor and Emotion: Language, Culture, and Body in Human Feeling* (Cambridge, 2000).

27. Hera Cook, 'Sense and Sensation: Controlling the Emotional Body in England 1940–1970', Paper for the ESSHC, 2008.

28. Gross, *Secret History of Emotions*, p. 110.

29. Kagan, *What Is Emotion?*, p. 4.

30. Ibid., p. 2.

31. Ibid., p. 27.

32. Ibid., p. 98.
33. Tomhave Blauvelt, *The Work of the Heart*, p. 8.
34. Ibid., p. 119.
35. Ibid., p. 195.
36. Ibid., p. 113.
37. For example Dylan Evans, *Emotion: A Very Short Introduction* (Oxford, 2003).
38. Quoted in Anna Green, *Cultural History* (Basingstoke, 2008), p. 119. Also see Daniel Lord Smail, *On Deep History and the Brain* (Berkeley and Los Angeles, CA, 2008).
39. Green, *Cultural History*, pp. 119–20.

BOOK REVIEWS

Clothing: A Global History, Or, The Imperialists' New Clothes. By Robert Ross. Cambridge: Polity Press. 2008. pp. 232. £15.99. ISBN 9780745631875.

This book from the Professor of African History at the University of Leiden ranges over 400 years of history and all five continents. It packs in a wealth of case studies of the ways that clothing has been used to define and to enforce identities at the interface between colonial and indigenous peoples. Ross is aware of the ways that religious, cultural and gender differences articulate clothing practice within societies, and that the personal and the political interact through dress. For example, he shows that leaders of newly independent West African states have tended to reject traditional clothing as too closely identified with particular tribes, and to adopt western-style business suits as a sign of their educated status. Conversely, visitors to Africa who adopt 'traditional' dress are likely to reveal not their knowledge of local practices but their lack of it, resulting in misunderstandings on both sides. These examples are drawn from a wide range of sources, both primary and secondary, and reference many texts that will be new to most readers.

The book is organized in chapters that start with the first colonial encounters in the seventeenth century, and end with the co-existence of 'alternate modernities' in the streets of London today. Within this broad timeframe, each chapter addresses a different theme, including Christian missions and clothing, and colonial nationalism. These are examined through case studies, each treated through a brief chronological survey and an account of the key points, making the text rather jumpy. Chapter 7 moves from southern Africa, to Australia, to the Pacific islands, then back to southern Africa, at different points in the nineteenth and twentieth century. This whistle-stop approach tends to undermine Ross's points about change and development within 'traditional' cultures.

Ross seeks to locate changes in non-western cultures against a background of change in western practices in the production and consumption of clothing. This is a key point, as colonialism acted as a vector for exporting goods as well as ideas to subject territories. However, the two chapters dedicated to western clothing (numbers 5 and 10) detract from the rest of the text. They summarize too briefly (and sometimes confusingly) material that is better covered elsewhere and reduce the space available for accounts of non-western dress.

Many of the examples Ross discusses are so complex that they would have repaid more detailed exegesis, such as the Herero of Namibia, whose western-style clothes were originally imposed by outsiders but were then internalized as an aspect of local identities. It would also have been interesting to have more discussion of the trade in garments and fabrics within colonial systems. This produced anomalies such as the 'shwe-shwe' fabric printed in Holland for South Africa which, after independence, was replicated in South African factories, where it is still being made. More attention to the

Cultural and Social History, Volume 6, Issue 4, pp. 517–534 © The Social History Society 2009

specific qualities of texture and pattern that enabled textiles to create meanings would have enriched Ross's historic narrative.

While Polity is to be congratulated for making the text available in paperback and at a reasonable price, there is evidence of some cost-cutting. There are only 16 images, several of which show large groups whose clothing is hard to decipher in small-scale reproductions. It is hard to follow Ross's accounts of unfamiliar clothing without visual prompts. Moreover, three of the illustrations are likely to be familiar to the reader from other texts: James Dean, Dior's 'New Look' and a 1910 corset advertisement. The odd choice of illustrations and the lack of detailed captions suggest that the images are an afterthought rather than an integral part of the text. There is also evidence of haste in the footnotes, where the names of cited authors are sometimes misspelt; this is particularly annoying as there is no separate bibliography for checking.

Clothing: A Global History contains a great deal of valuable information that is hard to find elsewhere, with extensive references that allow the reader to follow up topics of particular interest. Ross's focus on the cultural and political meanings of clothing will make it relevant to a wide range of courses. However, its compressed presentation of complex cases means that anyone intending to use it for teaching would be advised to back it up with some of the detailed studies Ross cites, or with a more visually literate text such as Margaret Maynard's *Dress and Globalisation* (Manchester University Press, 2004).

London Metropolitan University   CLARE ROSE
DOI 10.2752/147800409X467640

Information and Communication in Venice: Rethinking Early Modern Politics. By Filippo de Vivo. Oxford: Oxford University Press. 2007. pp. 312. £60.00. ISBN 9780199227068.

This impressive book is really two books in one. It is none the worse for that. On the one hand, it casts fresh light on one of the key political crises in the life of the Venetian Republic, the Papal Interdict of 1606–7, during which Venice and its territories were officially cut off from the Catholic World and the papacy and the Venetian government engaged in a public exchange of polemics to demonstrate that each was able of controlling the local population. On the other hand, the book explores the complex world of political communication in an early modern society and, in so doing, raises important questions about the ways in which information was acquired, disseminated and digested. Venice has long had a reputation as a society in which politics only directly concerned a very small proportion of the adult population, the patricians, who fiercely guarded sensitive information and used fear and censorship to deter all others from obtaining it. In an ironic methodological twist, De Vivo analyses the records of the *Inquisitori di Stato*, the magistracy responsible for running spies to monitor the views expressed by anyone outside the official discussions in government, and demonstrates that the much vaunted political secrecy of legend was anything but. Not only were government papers of all kinds circulated or mislaid by the functionaries who serviced the needs of government, but often the source of such information could be traced back to individual patricians who wished their ideas to have a wider circulation. Once such information had been released into the public domain, it spread widely, not only because of the omnipresence of gossip networks within Venetian society, but also because local and international politics engaged a broad social spectrum of people whose interest in politics scarcely conformed to the myth that it was a matter solely for patricians. Spies monitored pharmacies, particularly those close to the residences of foreign diplomats. It was well known that such establishments drew gatherings of customers who, while waiting for their purchases to be prepared, spent time in conversation about current politics and in reading newsletters from abroad. The discussion and transmission of political information in such contexts were far more than pecuniary transactions. Apothecaries and barbers used the availability of such information as a way of attracting customers to their shops, but there were many others – merchants, notaries, lawyers and business brokers – who needed to know what was going on as part of their work. Women, widely characterized by their male contemporaries as gossips, also participated in the diffusion of political information. The extent to which they did so was masked by the government spies' preoccupation with male subjects and deserves some further investigation.

De Vivo emphasizes the coexistence and interchange between oral and written forms of information. Both orality and literacy had their place in the circulation of information, whether it was official or unofficial. The texts of laws, which were posted up at key points in the city and its subsidiaries on the mainland so that they could be read by the populace, were also read out aloud by officials appointed for this purpose. Satires about issues and personalities of the day (often the work of highly educated authors) were posted up to be read and then repeated verbally, a process which also took place in reverse.

In 1968 William Bouwsma's magisterial study of the Venetian Interdict, *Venice and the Defense of Republican Liberty*, placed its emphasis on the ideological struggle between concepts of papal hegemony and the Republic's humanistic defence of its own liberty to function as a separate political entity. De Vivo's book enables us to return to the crisis from a new perspective. In some ways, it reverses the nature of the conflict by demonstrating how the Venetian Republic failed to constrain the circulation of subversive information or to control public discussion within the city itself. It argues that the crisis released political self-expression from below. The case is well made in the context of the book's general discussion of the organic way in which information circulated in oral and written forms. Ultimately, however, the two books do not entirely merge into one. In an epilogue, De Vivo makes the case that the resonances of the Interdict conflict among ordinary people continued into the seventeenth century, even if the flow of pamphlets declined with the resolution of the crisis. The implications of this book for long-term non-patrician politics in Venice deserve even more discussion than this.

Northumbria University

Alexander Cowan

DOI 10.2752/147800409X467659

The Family in Early Modern England. Edited by Helen Berry and Elizabeth Foyster. Cambridge: Cambridge University Press. 2007. pp. 244. £55.00. ISBN 9780521858762.

This collection of essays is dedicated to Anthony Fletcher, specifically selected to highlight his contribution to the field of early modern social history. Fletcher is cited as both teacher and mentor to the editors and the book includes a short biography commemorating his work to date. The collection also marks the thirtieth anniversary of the publication of Lawrence Stone's *The Family, Sex and Marriage, 1500–1800*, and each essay is inspired by a theme that Stone addressed in his research on family history.

Despite many of Stone's theories about the early modern family being subsequently criticized, the fact that this collection has been brought together as a result of his ideas suggests the impact of his work, even today. As expected, none of the essays pay lip-service to Stone's arguments, but use his theories as a starting point from which to broach the wider issues that surround the discussion of the family. The collection is designed to show the difficulty of imposing one collective ideal of 'the family' on the early modern experience, as Stone sought to do, as people fell within different categories of status, wealth and individual circumstances during their life cycle. In addition, the collection seeks to redress the imbalance that has been created by applying a distinction between 'gender' and 'family' history, to demonstrate the wider social and political connotations of 'family', by proposing new ideas and empirical sources for future research.

Tim Stretton, for example, argues that studies of the family and marriage have been hindered by concentrating on 'domestic' issues contained within church court material, suggesting that common law records also offer invaluable insights on problematic marriages, and that the common law was often more effective at resolving disputes than the Church. He also argues against Stone's idea that marriage bonds were at their peak of indissolubility between the Reformation and Restoration. Similarly, Garthine Walker argues against historians like Stone who have tended to associate the study of family and crime with 'domestic' issues, such as adultery or illegitimacy. Walker suggests that the tendency to prosecute the male householder over and above other members of his family has led to collective, family involvement in crime being overlooked. In particular, this has produced a 'gender-bias' as crimes such as scolding, slander and infanticide have become associated with women, whereas the wider world of criminal activity has been reserved for men. Using evidence relating to property crime, Walker's fascinating essay explains how families often acted together as a unit in the perpetration of crime.

Bernard Capp debates the impact of the Godly reforming campaign during the 1650s, which Stone termed 'Draconian', on both the community and the individual. In particular, Capp is interested in the extent to which the campaign was hindered or endorsed by popular support, proposing that the campaign was not such a grand failure as Stone had argued. Capp suggests that the level of popular antagonism towards reform in fact testifies to the success of the campaign within the parish.

John Walter's essay re-evaluates the composition of the 'crowd' during popular protest, taking issue with Stone's assumption that women engaged little in riots concerning state politics. He examines the social roles of protestors and the possibility that family priorities and strategies may have contributed to individual motivations to join the 'mob', as well as general social or class-related grievances. He further argues that people actively manipulated stereotypes of age or gender to justify or excuse involvement in protest. The theme of social negotiation and agency is expanded by Steve Hindle, who advocates the importance of petitions by or on behalf of the poor, in contrast to Stone's generalizations about the powerlessness and drudgery of the lower classes. The language and content of the petitions highlight the complexity of social negotiation and suggest the possibility that the poor may have exerted a degree of agency by playing on the paternalistic and reciprocal obligations that the governing classes were expected to fulfil. Few historians have exploited the role of petitioning in this way and Hindle rightly acknowledges their empirical value. A particular highlight is the essay by Berry and Foyster on childless men, which examines the role that the inability to have children played within the construction of masculine identities and children's importance in the emotional lives of early modern men. The final two chapters concentrate on the aristocracy, unlike the previous essays which consider the experience of lower to middling men and women. Ingrid Tague reconsiders Stone's assumptions about family patterns by evaluating how women perceived the boundaries of their families and their own role within them. Bailey, on the other hand, concentrates on child/parent relationships, which, she argues, have often been sidelined in the wider debate about the family.

Initially, I admit I was uninspired by both the title and the synopsis of this collection, expecting to find few ways to expand such clichéd debates. However, the essays are skilfully selected and unique, offering new and innovative avenues for future research and inviting further comment and exploration. This is an up to date and significant collection which brings the family firmly back to its rightful place at the heart of early modern social history, connecting the private sphere with the wider social and political debates of the time.

University of East Anglia   FIONA WILLIAMSON
DOI 10.2752/147800409X467668

The Origins of the Idea of the Industrial Revolution. By William Hardy. Oxford: Trafford Publishing. 2006. pp. 186. £10.99. ISBN 1412086809.

This book's title may not immediately strike its potential reader as sitting naturally in the sphere of social history. In truth, though, Hardy's short but nonetheless wide-ranging study of the development of the 'industrial revolution' idea is evidence of the increasingly porous nature of the boundaries between our sub-disciplines. This is far more than narrow intellectual history; it attempts to show how ideas of national industrial expansion and their spread were culturally generated and absorbed.

If David Cannadine's well-known study 'The Present and the Past in the English Industrial Revolution, 1880–1980' (*Past and Present*, ciii (1984), pp. 131–72) offered a picture of how Toynbee's concepts were subsequently used, transformed and fought over by historians and other public commentators, Hardy's book is its natural prequel. Boiled down, its concern is 'how did we arrive at Toynbee?' In answering that question, the author has scrupulously avoided the rather dull debate over the etymology of the phrase 'industrial revolution', preferring to examine how the context of Toynbee's model was fashioned in the century or so before his lectures. How, for example, Hardy asks, did the industrial revolution's widely recognized start date of 1760 (regardless of its objective accuracy) come to be so established? Why did elements like the swelling cotton sector and technological bursts assume such a dominant place in the national narrative? And what of the hackneyed descriptions of grim mills, social discontent, class antagonism, slum living and so on? From where did they emerge, in what ways were they spread, and how did they become incorporated into a 'standard' Toynbee-esque account?

These are important questions for social and cultural historians of the nineteenth century, for their answers help us to map the national framework of discussion. Its currents of communication, its public debates and its nexus between political, social, intellectual and industrial elites are all delineated here, but Hardy's work is particularly strong on how local experiences became co-opted into a grand national picture. The questions Hardy asks also, incidentally, demonstrate the importance of ideas in political and cultural debate and suggest that the nineteenth century was no more captivated by a bland managerial mindset than any period before or since.

So, sound questions are asked, but does the book deliver answers? On the whole, yes. It certainly shows how the language of technological breakthrough later employed in syntheses by Engels and Toynbee was being developed in elite enclaves like Parliament and Britain's many scientific and philosophical societies in the eighteenth century. Such tropes trickled out into wider public (largely middle-class) perceptions through periodicals, pamphlets, industrial tourism, and what might be called manufacturing travelogues. In passing, he also deals glancing blows to those, for instance, who still claim that protectionist Tories were at best uninterested in and at worst positively hostile to manufacturing's advance, or who assume that eighteenth and nineteenth century parliamentarians saw commerce and manufactures as hermetically discrete spheres. The book includes a splendid chapter on contemporary perceptions of social and moral decay and their relationship to the advance of industry. This contains – somewhat curiously – the best description I've read in short compass of the late eighteenth century 'contagion versus miasma' medical debate.

The volume, though, is slim and one is sometimes left wanting more. There is one useful chapter on the process by which elements as diverse as moral degeneration, social concern over working-class conditions, technology, the contribution of leading sectors, and the factory system were synthesized into an explanatory pattern, but there could easily have been more. Neither is this a book to pick up if one is interested in, say, the poor's perceptions of industrial change – but then the author does not claim that it contains any such insight. It is, rather, concerned with the components of a public idea that was essentially carried and contested by an educated social elite. A national conversation is examined, but Hardy makes it clear that it did not involve the whole nation. That, it has to be said, is not at all a weakness. Indeed, it is positively advantageous in a short volume to have that precision of focus.

It remains to be seen if Hardy's work will be picked up in the historiography of the industrial period – too frequently decent monographs from relatively unknown publishers fail to get wide recognition – but it surely deserves to be.

Open University   STUART MITCHELL
DOI 10.2752/147800409X467677

The Tichborne Claimant: A Victorian Sensation. By Rohan McWilliam. London: Hambledon Continuum. 2007. pp. 363. £25.00. ISBN 1852854782.

This book addresses a long-standing *cause célèbre* and seeks to explain not so much its enduring fascination as the reason why an incident which was, at one level, rather banal and comical was so significant and high profile in the minds of contemporaries. In doing so, McWilliam also demonstrates why it has continued to attract attention. Some people will wish to read this for information about the Tichborne tale, and they will not be disappointed: I do not know of a better and more detailed narrative assemblage of the whole sorry saga. The references are extensive, as is the bibliography, indicating the impressive research that has gone into this well-illustrated work. It is a maturely conceived and thoughtfully and lucidly written disquisition. McWilliam has put his story together not just in great depth but also with great breadth, and the end result justifies the time it has clearly taken to produce a work of genuinely outstanding scholarship.

In structuring his analysis as he does, McWilliam demonstrates a real comprehension of the nature of Victorian melodrama, thereby justifying his subtitle. The melodramas of the age (including the 'sensation novel') often included minutiae relating to the central figures in dramas and events initially apparently peripheral to the main narrative thread that are demonstrated in the denouement to be important elements in the morality that underpins the narrative. McWilliam mimics this process, but in a way that presents, for present-minded consumption, a complex and rich analysis of these various threads and how they were woven together at the time. But McWilliam does not make the classic error of seeking to include and explain all. Instead, he accepts and, more explicitly, points out to his readership that we will not fully understand the mosaic of the Tichborne case in terms of mentalities and attitudes. And while he is broad in his reach, there are aspects of the mosaic which are not really dealt with here: for instance, not all politically active working-class figures were sympathetic to either side in the Tichborne case.

The majority of working-class Victorians were not such serious types; they favoured a more popular type of political commentary on the world around them. As is shown by other surviving products of late Victorian working-class culture as well as the Tichborne ephemera included here, they had a taste for the titillating, the strange and the exotic. And what was more exotic than this imperially contextualized tale of (depending on which version you cared to believe) the return of a long-lost son, a scion of aristocracy who had experienced working-class realities in Australia and had become 'one of us' by marrying into the class; or the imposture of a first-class (and fat) scoundrel daring to try to deceive not just a forlorn mother but also the respectable and upper classes? Whichever side you took, it was an absorbing drama, especially when it was played out, twice, on one of the most popular stages of the day: the Victorian courtroom. There, the *dramatis personae* included figures already familiar to a newspaper-reading Victorian public. For the first (civil) trial, the Claimant had engaged 'Bally', Serjeant William Ballantine, a familiar and popular figure, known for his cross-examinations and flights of oratory. Facing Ballantine was Coleridge, the Solicitor General – whose involvement added gravitas to the proceedings – while the judge was the Chief Justice of the Common Pleas, Sir William Bovill. In the second (criminal) trial, there was the notoriously crotchety Alexander Cockurn, the Lord Chief Justice, whose involvement was likely to make for memorable interventions from the Bench presiding. Counsel for the prosecution, in this case, was Henry Hawkins – Hanging Hawkins as he was later dubbed – but Ballantine was replaced by Edward Kinealy, another familiar figure (he had prosecuted, for example, in the notorious Overend Gurney case, with its highly contemporary Northern Rock echoes). All this served to emphasize the human aspects of the events played out before the court, and McWilliam (while refusing to take either side and preferring to give as balanced an account as possible) never loses sight of this dimension. He thus provides an account which is readable because of the insights he adds to his analysis.

Some quibbles can be raised. For instance, from my perspective, while McWilliam provides a praiseworthy focus on the trials and seeks to contextualize them within the nineteenth-century criminal justice process, he has not fully comprehended the nuances involved; it is not always 'law-minded'. He does not, for instance, properly pick up on the weight given at the time to character testimony. And to describe Ballantine as taking a 'restrained' approach to advocacy when compared to Kinealy is to focus on the wrong dimension. *Both* men were perfectly capable of histrionics (just look at Bally's speeches in the Baroda case that McWilliam mentions!). But Ballantine was a good lawyer and worked with and within the law. Kinealy did not, and it was almost certainly on those grounds that the Claimant chose him to defend what was already, in purely legal terms, a pretty indefensible case.

The overall strength of the book is unmistakable. It does not just inform the reader about the Tichborne Claimant and the progress of his case until his final demise. It contextualizes it in the richness of its Victorian setting and comes as near to making sense of the whole nonsensical affair as could be achieved – and that turns it into a book which informs the reader about late Victorian British society, illuminating complex cultural agendas and often contradictory social rules, showing how these intersect and interact and how they affected popular understandings of many things. It is an admirable text for that – and it is also written in an enjoyably readable prose style.

Nottingham Trent University   JUDITH ROWBOTHAM
                                                        DOI 10.2752/147800409X467686

Free Trade Nation: Commerce, Consumption, and Civil Society in Modern Britain. By Frank Trentmann. Oxford: Oxford University Press. 2008. pp. xii + 450. £25.00. ISBN 9780199209200.

Free Trade Nation rides the crest of an ever-increasing wave of scholarly work on consumerism and its histories. The focus of this book is upon one aspect of this, the rise of free trade in the late nineteenth and early twentieth centuries and its subsequent decline and fall after the First World War. Trentmann's explanation for the success and failure of free trade differs significantly from those of others through the emphasis placed upon the role of the 'citizen-consumer'. This allows free trade to be thought of anew, not just as one of many economic policy choices facing politicians but as something with much deeper roots in civil society, as an idea and a way of life central to democratic culture and identity. Indeed, the crux of Trentmann's argument is that these robust foundations gave free trade an unassailable position in late Victorian and Edwardian Britain. In turn, Trentmann demonstrates how free trade faltered and fell as the interests of the citizen-consumer were redefined during and after the First World War.

The book, topped and tailed by an introduction and an epilogue, is divided into two parts of three and four chapters respectively. The first part discusses how the edifice of free trade was built up and maintained as a cornerstone of everyday life. It demonstrates how free trade became woven into the fabric of society and became indispensable through its appeal to people as citizen-consumers. The citizen-consumer came to represent the public interest, lending free trade an unrivalled legitimacy. The free trade message was delivered through a novel style of popular politics. This allowed it to attain a deep rootedness that made it possible for the liberal government to fend off Conservative appeals for tariffs in 1910. Indeed, free trade was able to survive despite increasing suspicions that Britain's commitment to unilateral free trade was becoming irrelevant in a world that lent evermore towards protection. The second part is concerned with the post-1914 erosion of free trade. Trentmann argues that the First World War was the key turning point in the fortunes of free trade. In doing so, he claims that other accounts have placed too great an emphasis on the depression from 1929 – rather, the rot had set in much earlier. The shock of wartime conditions acted as a catalyst for the reshaping of the citizen-consumer. Cheapness as a central legitimating link binding free trade with the consumer gave way to the importance of stability. As the interests of the consumer-citizen shifted, so did the parameters of the debate. Stability was to be attained through regulation rather than the free play of market forces. In this context, free traders found themselves increasingly marginalized. The last chapter, 'Final Days', which discusses Britain's switch from free trade to protection and preference from 1931, is significantly shorter than its predecessors. This is understandable. As Trentmann demonstrates, the damage had already been done.

One of the most notable achievements of this book is to show how free trade was apparent in people's everyday lives, how free trade was made material outside of arcane debate amongst politicians and economists. Indeed, Trentmann's argument rests upon demonstrating the ubiquity of free trade in terms of both who and where it reached. This he does by drawing upon an impressive and diverse array of sources. Cobden's ghost (projected by magic lantern!) appears in a 1909 adaptation of Charles Dickens' *A Christmas Carol* to remind a protectionist Scrooge and the audience of what they owed their untaxed dinners to (pp. 33–4, 123). In the summer of the following year free trade became a fixture on the promenade, as free trade lecturers headed to the seaside *en masse*, jostling for attention in Brighton, Morecambe and other popular resorts amongst the usual crowd of holiday attractions (pp. 109–16). The very materiality of the idea of free trade is enforced through a liberal use of illustrations, including a number of colour plates. In surveying the popular appeal of free trade, Trentmann skilfully and convincingly negotiates the thorny problem which has confronted many a scholar in attempting to gauge the impact of particular ideas or forces on society. To give just a single instance, though there is no oral testimony to attest to the success of the 'Free Trade shops', units hired to exhibit the benefits of free trade to passing shoppers, Trentmann offsets this through the use of reports made by local agents (p. 121).

Trentmann's epilogue highlights the lessons of his study for contemporary debates over trade liberalization and fair trade in the early twenty-first century, debates notable for their scant attention to history. Nevertheless, this book should find its way onto many a historian's bookshelf. The 'guide to further reading', a short essay in itself, that appears after the endnotes is a rollercoaster ride through an enormous literature that will be invaluable to those entering this area of study for the first time. For the already initiated, a web address is provided which allows access to a formidable 78 page bibliography. *Free Trade Nation* provides a new marker in the historiography of free trade and protection. But more than that, it demonstrates the need to blur the abstract boundaries between cultural, economic and political history as a way to finding more nuanced understandings of historical phenomena that were never so neatly demarcated.

University of Sheffield

PAUL ASHMORE
DOI 10.2752/147800409X467695

Anarchism, Revolution and Reaction: Catalan Labour and the Crisis of the Spanish State, 1898–1923. By Angel Smith. New York: Berghahn Books. 2007. pp. 405. £55. ISBN 9781845451769.

Until the 1990s, the predominant view of Spain's modern history was that it was marked by 'failure' and stood out as 'peculiar' in the western European context. The presence and persistence of a strong and active anarchist/anarchosyndicalist movement, especially in the country's industrial hub of Barcelona, was one of the key exhibits in this interpretation, and Spain's anarchists enjoyed a considerable amount of attention from historians, especially for their role in the Spanish Civil War.

The interest in anarchism has slackened in the past fifteen years or so. Spain's modern history has been reconceived as part of the European mainstream, no more peculiar than the history of any other western European country. Changes in historiographical interest, or fashion, have moved attention away from labour history and the Spanish Civil War, topics in which anarchism loomed large, to other areas, such as the Franco regime, where its importance was considerably less.

In this context, Angel Smith's book on the labour movement in Catalonia has something of a retro air. This does not, however, make it any less necessary or important because the question of why Spain – and especially Catalonia – was the locus of a powerful anarchosyndicalist union movement and marginal socialist and communist ones was never even close to being resolved. Smith's study may not turn out to be the last word on the subject, but he has advanced the discussion significantly.

Smith sets out to 'study the relationship between Catalan workers, the anarchosyndicalist movement and the development of the Spanish state' (p. 1) in the crucial period between 1898 and 1923, when the Restoration system established in 1875 was subject to the pressure of increasingly mass politics and eventually succumbed to Primo de Rivera's military coup. In doing so, he proposes to examine both the social history of labour and the political impact of labour organization. He also rejects the three prevailing interpretations of Catalan anarchism: the impact of immigrants from the rural south; the centrality of small-scale industry to anarchosyndicalist unions; and anarchism as part of a cross-class discourse in which the concerns of workers were not paramount. Smith's own view, based on a close social analysis of the development of Catalan industry and the community relationships to which it gave rise, is that anarchism was very much 'a movement based on industrial labour' and 'rooted in workers' real experience' (p. 5). Smith is fully aware of the various industrial ecologies within the region, and while Barcelona, understandably, receives the most attention, he is careful to describe developments outside the city, in the Freser and Ter Valleys and the Upper Llobregat.

One way in which Smith's book is definitely not retro is the attention he pays to gender, which becomes a central factor in the response of Catalan workers to the circumstances surrounding them. While labour unions and strikes continue to receive the lion's share of attention, they do not monopolize the argument; alongside them we also learn about such women-centred forms of protest as demonstrations against rising food prices, the influence of Church institutions and the Moroccan war.

Anarchism, Revolution and Reaction is divided into three sections. The first examines the roots of industrial militancy in Catalonia, including a chapter on 'gender, skill and class'. The key feature here is the specificity of Catalan industrial development. An economy dominated by textiles but which remained highly diverse presented the 'juxtaposition of a capitalist sector with the continuance of petty manufacture' (p. 32). Smith goes beyond the workplace experience of workers to examine residence patterns and neighbourhood relations as well as, crucially, the hostility of employers to unionization and the inability of the Spanish state to initiate some form of communication between the two groups. The state's failure to engage capital and labour in any meaningful form of discussion is one of the recurring motifs of the book.

Section two explores the 'Building of the Anarchist-Syndicalist Movement' in the crucial period between the loss of the last Latin American colonies in 1898 and the outbreak of the First World War. The key milestone is, of course, the creation of the

Confederación Nacional del Trabajo (CNT) in 1910. Much of this is well-known territory, but Smith does draw attention to the fact that pro-socialist unions were stronger in Catalonia than is usually assumed.

The final section analyses the trajectory of the CNT between 1915 and 1923. This was a particularly tumultuous period for Spain and it has been studied in considerable depth. Smith is good on the emergence of what he calls a 'terrorist wing' within the CNT (p. 249) and the internal divisions between advocates of violence, on the one hand, and more pragmatic union leaders such as Salvador Seguí, on the other. The end of the story is well known: in July 1923 General Miguel Primo de Rivera proclaimed a military dictatorship and banned the CNT.

Angel Smith has given us a thoroughly researched, highly detailed account of the birth and evolution of the Catalan labour movement, and especially of its powerful anarchosyndicalist wing, during a crucial quarter century of Spain's modern history. His book will be required reading for historians of twentieth-century Spain. It should also be on the reading list of any historian concerned with labour movements.

York University

ADRIAN SHUBERT
DOI 10.2752/147800409X467703

Cars for Comrades: The Life of the Soviet Automobile. By Lewis H. Siegelbaum. Ithaca, NY, and London: Cornell University Press. 2008. pp. 309. £20.50. ISBN 9780801446382.

Cars for Comrades is not just a major addition to the historiography of the USSR, but also a page-turning archaeology of the world of Chaikas, Volgas, Zhigulis and other famous marks. Lewis H. Siegelbaum has written several important studies on the industrial and labour history of twentieth-century Russia, and in this book he harnesses his considerable learning onto a great range of new material, producing a work that combines social, economic and cultural perspectives in a newly accessible and most refreshing way.

The first half of the book is a dissection of the three great sites of car production in the USSR. Siegelbaum devotes a chapter to each: the plant known variously as AMO, ZIS and ZIL in Moscow; the great GAZ factory in Gor'kii (the city which was Nizhnii Novgorod before 1932 and again after 1991; and the VAZ works in Togliatti. As he reminds us in such detail in one of his previous books, *Stakhanovism and the Politics of Productivity in the USSR, 1935-41* (Cambridge, 1988), industry was a particularly multifaceted activity in the Soviet Union. It brought together, more or less seamlessly, economic and political imperatives, while the diurnal relationship of worker to employer went far beyond work. An industrial enterprise, of which AMO/ZIS/ZIL, GAZ and VAZ were three behemoth-like examples, was charged not just with the production of a given good, but with directing much of the welfare and consumption that its employees enjoyed. Siegelbaum thus discusses the detail of particular cars that came out of each plant, the industrial context of their production, and the uses of foreign examples and investment (Togliatti, for instance, was the result of a deal with Fiat), as well as the lives of the workforce beyond the factory gate.

Both a weakness and a self-evident strength attach themselves to the structure of these chapters. Many of the same themes are considered separately in each, which can make it difficult for the reader to draw precise and quick thematic comparisons between the three centres of car production. Siegelbaum pays particular attention to housing, and while his material is relevant to a study of these industrial enterprises, it would not be out of place in another type of study; he does not always bring out what was particularly distinctive about the world of those who worked in the production of cars. Thus Siegelbaum writes about 'people's construction' in Gor'kii, whereby non-construction workers formed construction brigades and built apartment blocks in return for housing space, but does not tell us much about how car workers – as car workers, specifically – related to the task. He recounts a detailed story about a Togliatti woman enticed into marriage for the sake of her apartment, but provides insufficient context by which the reader might gauge its typicality, for car workers or Soviet citizens more generally.

A book of this ambition and wide range of sources will always be troubled by the representativeness of some of its evidence, and such stories, mined from the archives, act as rewarding glimpses of Soviet life rather than full-scale historical explanation. *Cars for Comrades* does, however, provide an overall analysis of how and why Soviet citizens related to cars in the way that they did, though one that is deliberately not animated by a single sustaining idea. In the second half of the book, Siegelbaum discusses roads, drawing on construction data and little known phenomena such as car rallies of the 1920s and 1930s, and relates his argument to the imperatives of Gulag slave labour and the government's consumption priorities. He goes on to consider literary representations, the economics of distribution and deficits, the multiple presences of the Soviet car along the boundary between public and private spheres, sport, masculinity, maintenance and ownership. He even takes some tentative steps towards the present day. The conceptual reach and empirical scope of this work allow Siegelbaum to go far beyond a re-creation of aspects of the Soviet experience, and to broach a full-throttle multi-explanation of how and why the Soviet car existed and developed as it did. He might have tied up the threads of his explanation more tightly in his conclusion, which acts instead as a post-Soviet epilogue, but then a work of this type is not designed to follow a single argument-ative line.

This book, with its impressive conspectus, rewarding analysis and broad foundation of evidence, still further burnishes Lewis Siegelbaum's distinguished reputation. It tells a story that fellow historians of the Soviet Union must read, but which will also be of interest to other historians of consumption and labour. Its accessible tone and sound structure make it immediately accessible to undergraduates, and it will be an inspiring addition to reading lists. Stripped of the economic detail, close historiographical analysis and occasional jargon that mark Siegelbaum's other major works, it will also be enjoyed by a wider history-reading public, and not just enthusiasts for automobiles. All readers will appreciate the pleasing illustrations, useful index, numerous endnotes (though not the absence of a bibliography), and the generally high standards of book production and reasonable price associated with this publisher.

University of Durham   MARK B. SMITH

DOI 10.2752/147800409X467712

Consuming Habits: Global and Historical Perspectives on How Cultures Define Drugs. Edited by Jordan Goodman, Paul E. Lovejoy and Andrew Sherratt. London and New York: Routledge. Second edition 2007. pp. 283. ISBN 0415425816 (hbk).

Heroin: The Treatment of Addiction in Twentieth Century Britain. By Alex Mold. DeKalb: Northern Illinois University Press. 2008. pp. 236. ISBN 9780875803869.

When *Consuming Habits* was first published in the mid-1990s, based on an earlier 1991 *Past and Present* conference on ' Peculiar substances', its broad approach to the study of mind-altering substances, rooted in cultural and economic history and in anthropology, was unusual. Such distinctiveness is now less the case. Research on the history of substance use has mushroomed; coverage of a range of substances has diversified. It is much more common now for substances like tobacco or alcohol to be discussed together with illicit drugs, rather than separately.

Nevertheless, a reissue and revision of the earlier book is welcome. This second edition has two additional chapters. James Mills covers the internationalization of trading in cannabis from the nineteenth century into the twentieth. He locates this spread of the cannabis market in part to the demand provided by the indentured Indian labour system, which located cannabis consumers throughout the colonies. The other new chapter, by Axel Klein and Susan Beckerleg, examines the current production and consumption of khat. Khat, unlike many substances which have made the transition across national trading boundaries, has become an internationalized commodity without further production processes or the development of a more specific alkaloid. Its use has thus remained concentrated in immigrant communities in European countries and has not spread to the wider population. The contemporary debates round this drug and its status provide an interesting illustration of the forces which define what counts as a drug or as a food/vegetable and whether or how it becomes the subject of regulation.

The other chapters in the book, some of which appear to have been revised and some not, are familiar. They are wide ranging: from Stephen Hugh Jones' careful analysis of the ways in which the Barasana, a group living in northwest Amazonia, use coca and how this has affected concepts of food and non-food, to Jordan Goodman's study of the Europeanization of what he calls 'soft drugs' – tea, coffee, chocolate and tobacco – in the eighteenth century. Goodman is here drawing attention to a process which transformed modes of consumption in the host countries and which saw these substances substituted for other European plants.

The late Andrew Sherratt wrote the valuable introduction to the first edition and this is reproduced here. Sherratt's insistence that 'peculiar substances' should be treated within a common framework, and that categories such as 'drug' and food' are culturally and historically constructed, was ground breaking, not least for his elegance of expression. His comments have largely stood the test of time, but time has also brought some change. The comment that 'Some once widely consumed substances, such as cannabis, have crossed the line and been classified as dangerous drugs …; others, like tobacco, have not' (p. 2) produces a wry smile in 2008.

The bibliography has to some extent been updated, but it is disappointing that the remaining editors have not taken the opportunity of a new edition to make more substantial revisions to their own concluding comments. The questions raised by this collection – looking across the substances, for example, or the relative impact and rationale of taxation or monopoly based systems of substance regulation – could speak to the present. Such an addition could have built on and developed Sherratt's introduction.

Alex Mold's history of heroin addiction treatment in Britain presents new research. The book is based on Mold's PhD thesis, which analysed the development of treatment in Britain from the 1960s to the 1980s, and this has been expanded to take account of the earlier decades from the 1920s, with a brief survey of the post-1980s debates. To any historian of drug policy, this is a not unfamiliar story. The Rolleston Report of the 1920s established the so-called 'British system' of drug treatment involving the recognition of addiction as a disease requiring maintenance treatment. This pact between primarily middle-class addicts and their doctors lasted until the 1960s, when the changing profile of drug use brought an altered medical response.

What followed over the next decades provides the core of this book. The second Brain report of 1965 took addiction treatment out of the hands of general practice and located it in hospital based Drug Dependence Units (DDUs), run by consultant psychiatrists. Early heroin prescribing and the continuation of the Rolleston maintenance formula gave way, by the end of the 1970s, to a reliance on methadone, the synthetic opiate, and a strict 'one size fits all' model of abstinence as a goal. London based consultant psychiatrists operated to a group formula, enforced through clinical guidelines, which imposed this model on reluctant addicts. The main locus of opposition was in private practice. In the 1980s a series of GMC cases sought to discipline one of the main private practice prescribers, Dr Anne Dally, and this tactic ultimately succeeded.

Alongside this assertion of a specialized medical response, a wider 'policy community' around drugs had been developing, arguing for the concept of 'problem drug use' rather than addiction or dependence. The advent of HIV/AIDS and the fear that drug use might be a bridge for the virus to spread into the general population represented a golden opportunity for this approach to gain credibility. The 'new dawn' of HIV led to a focus on effective treatment as a goal. The Labour government in the 1990s then linked treatment with crime reduction. 'Treatment works' was the cry; but it worked, so researchers argued, in reducing crime, and thus had political utility. Mold ends with the current resurgence of enthusiasm for abstinence, another twist in the story, a reaction to the perceived 'dead end' of methadone maintenance. The complexity of addiction treatment and of the 'condition' with which it purports to deal will continue.

The book's strength is twofold. Firstly, there is its tone: this is properly historical, judicious, assessing different interpretations, locating its subject material in wider contexts of research on the development of health services in this period or in the extension of the medical 'gaze'. That type of approach is still uncommon enough in the history of substance use for its appearance in this book to be applauded. It is also research based, making good use of the Ministry of Health archives on the Brain reports and the Dally archive at the Wellcome Library. It is a pity that some of the key players still around were not interviewed, but Mold nevertheless weaves her way deftly through areas which have occupied controversialists in the different drug camps, producing a synthesis which is both plausible and readable.

Taken together the two books show much that is best about current histories of 'peculiar substances', not least that they approach this area in such very different but equally valuable ways.

London School of Hygiene and Tropical Medicine,   VIRGINIA BERRIDGE
University of London   DOI 10.2752/147800409X467721

African American Theater: A Cultural Companion. By Glenda Dicker/sun. Cambridge: Polity Press. 2008. pp. 210. £18.99. ISBN 9780745634432.

Until quite recently, the history of the American theatre attracted only limited scholarly attention. Over the last twenty years, however, scholars working in a range of fields have begun to explore the significance of the theatre both as a key economic institution and as an arena in which important debates about race, class, gender and national identity have played themselves out. What was once a quiet crossroads where literature met theatre arts is now a bustling intersection where various academic disciplines converge in new and exciting configurations. Strategically located at the hub of this intersection, Glenda Dicker/sun's interactive guide to the theatrical traditions of African Americans is an interesting and often very challenging contribution to a body of scholarship that has transformed how we view theatrical entertainment in the United States.

Taking as her central metaphor the myth of the people who could fly, Dicker/sun traces the struggle of African Americans to express themselves creatively from the era of slavery, when they were symbolically shorn of their wings, to the present, when they are once again free to take to the sky. In the process, she explores how the African-American experience has been variously represented on the stage, introducing her reader to a wide range of black dramatists and performers. Some of them – Josephine Baker, Zora Neale Hurston, Paul Robeson, Lorraine Hansberry, Amiri Baraka and August Wilson, for example – are well-known figures. Others, such as James Weldon Johnson, Mary Burrill and Theodore Brown, are rather more obscure but, as Dicker/sun demonstrates, no less worthy of our attention. Dicker/sun's book is far more than simply an overview of the history of African-American theatre, however. It also functions as a guide for theatre practitioners, pointing aspiring actors and dramatists towards primary source materials and suggesting ways in which they might engage with them creatively.

For all its strengths, though, Dicker/sun's book is fraught with problems. Dicker/sun's strategy of framing the narrative in mythic terms, for instance, works reasonably well as long as Dicker/sun is in a storytelling mode, but as soon as she attempts to deploy the archetypes she identifies in historically specific contexts it lets her down. Her comments on the significance in African-American folk culture of trickster figures such as Brer Rabbit, Slave John and Stagolee, for example, are well made. But, in the absence of detailed discussion of the relationship between black performance styles and black politics, her attempts to link these archetypes to political activists like Huey Newton and Malcolm X and popular entertainers like Whoopi Goldberg and Richard Pryor fall flat. To complicate matters still further, the text is punctuated with factual errors. Some of these are relatively minor and might easily have been picked up in the proof-reading/fact-checking process – for example, John Singleton is mistakenly identified as the director of the Hughes Brothers' 1993 film *Menace II Society*. Others are rather more serious and bespeak major gaps in the author's knowledge of the African-American past. Perhaps the most jarring is Dicker/sun's repeated use of the term "Exodusters" to describe the hundreds of thousands of African Americans who migrated from the rural South to the urban North in the early twentieth century. Not only is she applying an entirely inappropriate label to one group of black migrants. She is also erasing from the historical record another group – the freed slaves who travelled from the old slave states of the South to Kansas and points west in the late 1870s – to whom it might legitimately be applied.

What is most troubling about this book, however, is that Dicker/sun chooses to define her readership in racially exclusive terms. In her introduction, for example, she encourages her readers to compile what she terms a "Black Life Book" – a scrapbook recording family stories, important dates, key life events, etc. – and at the end of each chapter she sets out a series of exercises designed to facilitate this process. Whilst it might be argued that anyone, regardless of race or ethnicity, could usefully take part in these exercises, it seems unlikely that Dicker/sun would be comfortable with the idea of white students donning Afro wigs to perform the work of black poets, playwrights and musicians. The goal of fostering cultural pride amongst young African Americans is a laudable one. But as an educator who teaches students from a wide range of racial and ethnic backgrounds, I would hesitate to assign a text that allows this objective to take priority over other, more inclusive ways of thinking about the African-American past.

Brunel University

Sean P. Holmes

DOI 10.2752/147800409X467730

Karl Marx, Anthropologist

Thomas C. Patterson

"This is a timely reminder of both the Enlightenment background and holistic nature of Marx' anthropology, which concerns not merely understanding classical industrial capitalism but also such diverse issues as the modern age of empire, human origins and non-Western political systems'.

Dr Nikolai Ssorin-Chaikov, University of Cambridge

After being widely rejected in the late 20th century the work of Karl Marx is now being reassessed by many theorists and activists. *Karl Marx, Anthropologist* explores how this most influential of modern thinkers is still highly relevant for Anthropology today.

Marx was profoundly influenced by critical Enlightenment thought. He believed that humans were social individuals that simultaneously satisfied and forged their needs in the contexts of historically particular social relations and created cultures. Marx continually refined the empirical, philosophical, and practical dimensions of his anthropology throughout his lifetime.

Assessing key concepts, from the differences between class-based and classless societies to the roles of exploitation, alienation and domination in the making of social individuals, *Karl Marx, Anthropologist* is an essential guide to Marx's anthropological thought for the 21st century.

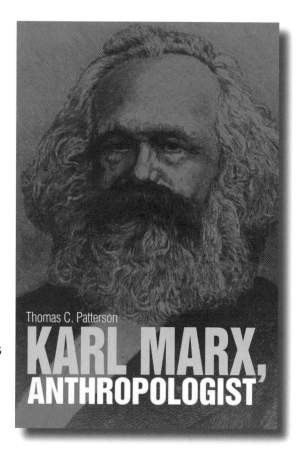

AVAILABLE APRIL 2009 - ORDER ONLINE AT WWW.BERGPUBLISHERS.COM

April 09 • 256pp • 234 x 156 mm
PB 978 1 84520 511 9 **£19.99 $34.95**
HB 978 1 84520 509 6 **£55.00 $109.95**

CULTURAL & SOCIAL HISTORY

NOTES TO CONTRIBUTORS

SUBMISSION GUIDELINES

Submissions to *Cultural and Social History* should be sent in electronic format. To submit a manuscript electronically, please send it either in WORD or in RICH TEXT FORMAT to **culturalsocialhistory@bergpublishers.com**. All submissions should include a 100 word abstract and four to five keywords.

Copies of any statistical tables, maps, or illustrations that cannot be sent electronically should be sent to *Cultural and Social History*, c/o Centre for Contemporary British History, Institute of Historical Research, Senate House, Malet Street, London WC1E 7HU, UK. Provide your name(s), address(es) and contact information on a separate title page. Articles should be no more than 9,000 (inclusive of notes). The total word count should be added at the end of the manuscript.

Reviews and review articles should be submitted direct to the Book Review Editor.

LAYOUT

All material should be formatted for A4 or quarto paper, in double-spaced typing. Ample margins should be left. Each page of the typescript should be numbered. Notes should be kept to a minimum, and supplied as endnotes. They should be numbered consecutively and double-spaced, beginning on a new page at the end of the article. **Please do not use any endnote/footnote formatting which may be available with your software**. Please avoid cross-references as far as possible.

In Reviews, all material should be incorporated into the text: there should be no endnotes. In Reviews, the author's name should appear at the end of the review, together with the name of his/her institution.

SPELLING AND PUNCTUATION

Please use UK English spelling and punctuation. In general, *The Concise Oxford Dictionary* is our arbiter of spelling, especially for hyphenated words, words in italics, etc. Use 'z' spelling for all words ending in '-ize', '-ization' (organize, organization). However, alternative spellings in quoted material, book and article titles should not be changed. We also recommend *The Oxford Dictionary for Writers and Editors* and *Hart's Rules* (both published by Oxford University Press) as useful reference works.

Please see the website http://www.bergpublishers.com/JournalsHomepage/CulturalandSocialHistory/JournalMenu/AuthorGuidelines/tabid/3510/Default.aspx for full details regarding which conventions to use.

FIGURES AND ILLUSTRATIONS

It is the author's responsibility to clear any necessary permissions for artwork he/she wishes to include.

Artwork MUST be submitted with the final draft of the article. Please note that while Berg Publishers will make every effort to ensure that your artwork is carefully handled and returned to you as soon as possible, artwork must, of necessity, be sent out of house and we can accept no responsibility for loss or damage. Therefore, we suggest that you if your artwork is irreplaceable DO NOT send us the originals.

Instead images should be submitted on disk or via email as either TIFFS or JPEGS (scanned at 300 dpi for photographs/half tones and 600 dpi for maps, line drawings or artwork containing text). Images embedded in Word documents can NOT be used. Similarly, graphics downloaded from Web pages are not acceptable for print reproduction. These graphics are low-resolution images (usually 72 dpi) that are suitable for screen display but far below acceptable standards for print reproduction.

The numbering on the artwork must be clearly marked, as must its position on the manuscript. Keep artwork separate from the text, with the figure number penciled in on the back of each figure. A separate list of captions and copyright information etc. should also be included. Although the print version of the journal will ordinarily only reproduce images in black and white, authors are encouraged to submit artwork in colour, since images will be available in colour in the online version of the journal. There is, however, a small budget for reproducing colour illustrations in print. Authors should liaise with the editors about any plans to include illustrations in colour in the print version of the journal.

NOTES AND REFERENCES

Use the short-title system of referencing for endnotes. Provide a full reference in the form of a note in the first instance, and thereafter a shorter version of the title should be used. Do not use 'op. cit'.

1. Mary Hamer, *Writing by Numbers: Trollope's Serial Fiction* (Cambridge, 1987), p. 25.

...

3. Hamer, *Writing by Numbers*, p. 27.

COPYRIGHTS

In submitting an article to **Cultural and Social History** an author recognises that, on its acceptance for publication, its exclusive copyright shall be assigned to the Social History Society and operated on the Society's behalf by the publisher. The publisher will not put any limitation on the freedom of the author to use material contained in the article in other published works of which he/she is author or editor. It is the author's responsibility to obtain permission to quote material from copyright sources.